LOOKING AND FINDING

'There are ninety-nine things to be done, or nine hundred and ninety-nine, whether you live in a town and go sometimes to the country or the sea, or whether you live in the country and go sometimes to the town.'

Geoffrey Grigson's moral is –
don't stay at home, but go and explore.
Don't stay indoors, but go and look.

This book is about looking – and finding. Anybody, if he takes the trouble, and looks in the right place, can find chipped flints, a badger skull, or pieces of pottery three thousand years old – though he might find a treasure ship as well, if he gets up, and goes out, and looks. Who knows?

THE SECONDHAND BOOKSHOP

Geoffrey Grigson

Looking and Finding

and
Collecting and Reading
and Investigating and
Much Else

Drawings by
Christopher Chamberlain,
Sheila Stafford and John Pezare

Carousel Editor: Anne Wood

TRANSWORLD PUBLISHERS LTD
A National General Company

LOOKING AND FINDING

A CAROUSEL BOOK 0 552 54007 2

Originally published in Great Britain
by John Baker (Publishers) Ltd.

PRINTING HISTORY
John Baker edition published 1958
John Baker revised and enlarged edition published 1970
Carousel edition published 1971
Carousel edition reprinted 1971

For
All of you including
HESTER, SOPHIA, FRANCES
and FRANCES and JOSEPH

Carousel Books are published by Transworld
Publishers Ltd.,
Cavendish House, 57–59 Uxbridge Road,
Ealing, London W.5

Made and printed in Great Britain by
Cox & Wyman Ltd., London, Reading and Fakenham

CONTENTS

ILLUSTRATIONS

A WORD TO BE READ FIRST

Nature hath furnished one part of the earth, and man another. The treasures of time lie high, in urns, coins, and monuments, scarce below the roots of some vegetables. Time hath endless rarities, and shows of all varieties; which reveals old things in heaven, makes new discoveries in earth, and even earth itself a discovery.

SIR THOMAS BROWNE

A WORD TO BE READ SECOND

THERE are ninety-nine things to be done, or nine hundred and ninety-nine, whether you live in a town and go sometimes to the country or the sea, or whether you live in the country and go sometimes to the town.

This book is about a few of them, including some (I hope) you have never thought of.

Unless you count shells and skulls, natural history does not really come in. It does look in now and again through the door. But there are already scores of books about natural history.

This book begins with maps and ends with museums, in particular your own museum. In the common sense, though, not everything this book is about, can be collected. So don't misunderstand if I say that our heads are also museums – of the best kind. I mean they are places where things we cannot possess, and ideas and knowledge we can possess, are stored.

Another thing. I do not expect that everybody is going to develop into an expert. There isn't any need to do everything in imitation of experts or *too* seriously.

It is not a bad thing to give yourself pleasure and delight, so long as your pleasures and delights do not get in the way of other people or upset them.

It is not a bad thing to be inquisitive and to wonder.

I hope this is a book of wonders,
as well as a book against
having nothing to do.

A SHELF OF MAPS

ONE morning after a storm, in 1831, a fisherman on the Isle of Lewis noticed a hole in a sandbank which had been eaten into by the sea. He looked; and there in the sand he found a small square box of slabs of stone. He lifted up the slab on top, and dropped it, and ran home and told his wife he had found a nest of demons out on the beach.

CHESSMEN OF WALRUS IVORY

'Go and look again,' said his wife, who had more sense. 'There might be gold.'

He went back, put his hands into the box and drew out a bearded king, four inches high, with a sword across his lap; then a knight on horseback, then bishops and soldiers and queens, until nearly a hundred small pink creatures lay on the sand.

They were not demons, but chessmen; carved out of the ivory tusks of morse, or walrus, seven hundred years before. And today, kings and queens and courtiers and army, they sit in row after row in a glass case in the King Edward VII Gallery in the British Museum, in London.

I used to look at them and say to myself, what luck! – and ask why everyone else had luck and found things, and why all the things worth finding were already on the other side of the glass where they couldn't be touched – these rare and wonderful chessmen, or a skull made of rock crystal, or a gold cup out of a barrow.

But it wasn't luck, entirely. The fisherman was out on the beach after the storm. He was looking for things, though not for demons in a stone box; he was hoping for a good log or a plank or a drowned body with rings on its fingers and a gold watch in its waistcoat pocket, or a barrel of wine, or a dead whale. He was out and about and deserved his luck. He was looking for one thing and found another.

Moral: don't stay at home, but go and explore. Don't stay indoors, but go and look.

This book is about looking – and finding. It is about a great many things which are worth finding, even if they would not all fit into glass cases in the British Museum, or on to the shelves of your own museum.

Anybody, if he takes the trouble, and looks in the right place, can find chipped flints instead of gold cups, a badger skull instead of a crystal skull, or pieces of pottery three thousand years old instead of all the ship treasure of Sutton Hoo – though he might find another ship treasure as well, if he gets up, and goes out, and looks. Who knows?

If you explore round your home, in the town or in the country, at home or on holiday, you need maps, that is certain; and here you are lucky because the maps of England, Wales, Scotland and Ireland, more than maps of any other country, are like books in themselves, full of information. There is a good deal of explorer's information, first of all, on the Ordnance Maps, which you can buy in the stationer's shop – the maps of one inch to a mile, one inch on the paper to one mile outside the front door.

If you live in the middle of a sheet – that will be more luck – miles and miles of country will spread all round you on the map; which will tell you where to find such desirable things to know and explore as:

Old roads	Canals in use
Roman roads	Canals disused
Green lanes	Fords
Footpaths	Footbridges
Old railways	Ferries

It will guide you to:

Churches with square towers	Windmills
Churches with spires	Watermills
Castles and ruins	Burial mounds
Ancient chapels	Burial chambers
Ancient houses	Camps and forts
Follies and monuments	Standing stones
Dovecotes	Deserted villages
Barns	Battlefields
Pounds	Old mines and mineheaps

It will guide you to things so explorable as:

Gravel pits	Springs
Old quarries	Streams
Cliffs	Rivers
Rocks	Weirs
Gorges and glens	Waterfalls
Caves	Woods
Sandhills	Marshes
Pools	Wildernesses
Ponds	Rough pastures
Dewponds	Fossil forests

It will direct you up to high places and tell you how high they are above the sea (you find the heights printed in black figures on the map; and for every height there will be, if you look, a 'bench-mark' on the ground, a line and a broad arrow – a government arrow – cut into the rock or into a wall). The map, too, will mark the boundaries of your own parish, and your own country; and will give you names of hills and hamlets and villages and farms – which have meanings to be discovered.

One small square inch on the map, though, is very little compared to one large square mile on the ground. A one-inch map cannot mark everything, it cannot include every name. Also there is no room on these maps, since they are so crowded, for you to write in, as you should, extra names and extra objects, which will be of concern to yourself as you explore and discover.

Bigger maps. Probably they will not sell them in the shop where you bought the one-inch map. Ask for them as birthday presents, or send away for them yourself (see the end of the chapter). The next size gives more room, more facts, more names – one mile of countryside or town reduced, this time, not to an inch on the map, but to about $2\frac{1}{2}$ inches; one square mile of countryside reduced to a square on the map of which each side is about $2\frac{1}{2}$ inches long.

That is better. On this $2\frac{1}{2}$ inch map very thin grey lines actually mark the limits of every field. You will find your own house, your own garden, or paddock, or your own orchard. Specks of blue will mark quite tiny ponds and pools.

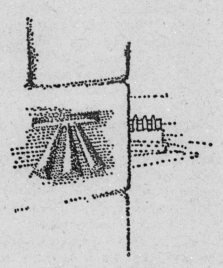

A BENCHMARK

Then, bigger still, maps of six inches to the mile, with still more names and facts, still smaller things clearly shown. Of course, as the scale of the map gets larger, so each sheet, each individual map (they cannot be enormous), covers fewer and fewer miles; and you will probably want more and more sheets. From the centre of a $2\frac{1}{2}$ inch map, you go about three miles each way to the edge. The six-inch maps cover six square miles on every sheet, giving a much smaller walk or bicycle ride from the centre; but much more empty white space for writing in your own discoveries.

Everyone (I think) should quite fearlessly write on his own maps. Six-inch maps are small enough to take with you, rolled up. If you want to, you can add things out of doors in pencil, and then write them in more carefully at home. In Indian ink, though; not the ordinary ink of a fountain pen, which would run and make a mess if the map were taken out again, and splashed in a shower.

After six inches to the mile, the next jump is bigger still, to sheets 25 inches to the mile. They are best of all if you want to have in front of you, as big and bold as possible, say, your own garden, or a most particular field or corner.

H. G. Wells once wrote a story about a Time Machine, which could take travellers back and back and still further back into the centuries. Old maps are Time Machines. In a secondhand bookshop it is sometimes possible to buy old ordnance survey maps, one inch to the mile, of the very first edition. (A publisher, David and Charles, is now reprinting them.)

The surveyors, making these maps for the army (or more exactly for the Ordnance, which was the department of stores for the army, in the Tower of London), took nearly a hundred years to cover all of England, Wales, Ireland, Scotland and the islands; but in the corner of some of their first maps you will see, neatly engraved in copperplate, that they were published at the Tower by Lieutenant-Colonel Mudge (who directed the surveyors) as early as 1809 or 1813.

To go for a walk on one of these first ordnance survey maps is to walk in the country more than a hundred years ago, before the Battle of Waterloo. Though the first surveyors did not put into the maps as much as modern map-makers or cartographers, you soon realize how many changes there have been. You may notice on the old map a small village or a farmstead, a windmill or a withy-bed which does not exist any more.

You may see that a familiar bluebell wood was not even planted in 1809; you may see (this is more likely) that a wood once grew at some place where you may still be able to pick wood anemones in a corner of an open field. You may see there was a cottage once on a piece of humpy ground where snowdrops endure from the old garden, or that there was once a barn at the end of an overgrown lane.

The map may give the name of this lost barn – if it had a name.

One secret is not known to everybody. Many of the drawings which the surveyors made still exist. Often these are on a larger scale than the published map, often they include a detail of something vanished and gone which was never printed on the maps. For very little money, you can buy a photostat of one of these drawings if you write to the Map Room at the British Museum.

Have a look, certainly, at the old coloured county maps which are often framed and hung on the wall. They may go back to Queen Elizabeth I's time; but they will not help you very much. The scale will be too small; and these cartographers contented themselves with including little more than rivers and the bigger roads and names of towns and villages. Also they did not draw their maps very accurately.

Are you on good terms with the vicar or rector? If you are, you might ask him if he still has in his house one of the huge parish maps made just over a hundred years ago, called Tithe Apportionment Maps. It will be drawn by hand, not printed; sometimes there will be a pen-and-ink or a watercolour picture, in one corner, of the church

or the village as it used to look; and the map will be huge
enough for a crawl. My father was the vicar of our
parish. We used to borrow the Tithe Map, spread it out
on the floor – nearly the whole floor – of the spare room,
and crawl about it by the hour looking for vanished
tracks, footpaths, cottages, mills, and salmon-weirs on
the river.

Often, though, these tithe maps can only be seen now
in some central storage place in your county or diocese;
or in an office in London, in Finsbury Square (the office
of the Tithe Redemption Commission); which is a pity,
at any rate from the explorer's point of view.

What else is worth having or seeing?

Charts, and a number of extra-special Time Machines from the Ordnance Survey.

If you live on the coast or go to the sea for holidays,
you can do with old Admiralty charts from a secondhand bookshop, or modern Admiralty charts. They
are especially good for islands.

A bookshop selling new books can probably provide
the extra-special (but rather small-scale) Time Machines, one of which (in two sheets, for north and for
south) whizzes you back to Monastic Britain, to Britain
of the monks and friars and nuns between 1066 and 1540
– that's to say between William the Conqueror's
conquest and the time when the abbeys and priories
'with their golden glittering tops' were pulled down or
closed down.

Another of these Time Machines of the Ordnance
Survey (in two sheets as well) whizzes you back still
further into the Dark Ages, between 871, which is the
year when Alfred became king of England, and 410,
which is when the Romans left; and a third one (in a
single sheet) presents everything about Roman Britain –
Roman towns and forts and marching camps and signal

stations, temples and villas (which were the headquarter houses of big Roman estates) and roads and canals and mines and potteries and places where they boiled salt out of sea-water; everything from the mines at Dolaucothi in Wales, where they dug for gold, to the lighthouse, still standing above the sea at the town they called Dubris and we call Dover.

If you have anything Roman in your neighbourhood, it will be there, I am pretty certain, on that map of Roman Britain. And last there is a map of Ancient Britain, in two sheets, north and south, containing everything archaeologically visible and important which is older than A.D. 1066.

Also a geological map, one sheet for Scotland and the far north, one for Wales and the rest of England, each as gay as a box of watercolours – a map of all rocks visible or invisible, from chalk to granite.

There you have your library of maps, better than any explorer has ever had before; ready to guide you to all the most excellent, outlandish and impossible places for picnics of the right kind (which never are the right kind unless they have an object in view; and which should be in any place from the top of a church tower to the comfortable – or uncomfortable – fork of a tree).

Buy your one-inch maps on paper, not cloth. The paper maps do not cost so much. To make them last longer you can paste them down yourself on to butter muslin. Or, stronger still, you might find in your house a spare piece of terylene curtain-net.

Bigger Ordnance Survey maps – they are not at all expensive – and the many-coloured maps of the Geological Survey you can buy from the bookshops of the Stationery Office in London (49 High Holborn, W.C.1 and 423 Oxford Street, W1), or from Stationery Offices in Edinburgh, Manchester, Birmingham, Cardiff, Bristol, and Belfast. Or you can write for them to Edward Stanford, Ltd, 12 Long Acre, London, WC2.

The northern and southern sheets of the double maps I have mentioned can be bought separately.

For Admiralty charts write to J. D. Potter, 145 Minories, London, EC3.

You remember those chessmen at the beginning of the chapter, in the British Museum, from the Isle of Lewis?

You can buy reproductions of them, from pawn to knight, bishop, castle, queen and king, and though they are made of a hard plastic resin they look very like the originals. Only I warn you, they are not cheap. It would be a question of getting one at a time, if you ever think of having the set.

2

A SHELF OF BOOKS
INCLUDING TWO IN PARTICULAR

FIND if you can – but when you have found, you want
to know what you have found.

So this is a short chapter strictly about books, bookshops, and libraries. Skip it if you want to go ahead to
more practical stuff about finding. But spare time for
this chapter later on, and come back to it. I shall remember to remind you.

Generally (there may be exceptions) librarians do not
bite; nor do secondhand booksellers. Librarians want
to help, secondhand booksellers want to be helped. You
help them if you buy their books. And you help librarians in the public library if you give them a chance
to feel they are helping you.

So have no fears of public library or secondhand bookshop. March in. Ask where the local books are or the
books about collecting; and look.

There are books about most things, most counties and
many places – possibly about the place or the town or
even the parish you live in. I know a book, you would
scarcely think it existed, about the delights of eating
young pink moles dug up from the ground or very young
pink rats pulled out of a stack of wheat (doubtful delights, but then the book was written during the First
World War when the writer thought that everyone was
going to starve). I know another book listing all the wild

flowers which grow on the ruins of the Colosseum in
Rome.

There are scores of books – as you would expect, and
you may have some of them – on such things as
Butterflies and Moths and Birds and Birds' Eggs and
Wild Flowers and Ferns and Funguses; which are not
the concern of this book.

There are books you might not expect – breathe
deeply and read the whole list aloud without stopping –
on Flints, Farms, Fields, Fossils, Villages, Bridges,
Roads, Roman Roads, Coins, Canals, Cliffs, Caves,
Mines, Mazes, Dewponds, Barrows (which are burial
mounds), Abbeys, Castles, Things Carved in Church,
Monuments in Church, Holy Wells, Bygones, Seals off
old Wine Bottles (which you may be lucky enough to
find), Dialects, Names of Places, English Earthquakes,
Firemarks, Weathercocks, Sundials, Windmills; quite a
number of which *are* the concern of this book.

Useful, but you cannot own them all. Public libraries
have many of them. Public libraries, too, will have
county histories (look up your own town or parish in the
index), and books about local buildings, and dialect dictionaries, and all the volumes of the magazine – if one
exists – published by your own county's archaeological
and natural history society. They will have the books
which are far too difficult to find or too expensive to buy,
old ones and new ones, large ones and small ones, ones in
twenty volumes and ones in twenty pages – the books
about archaeology and local history, and local arts, and
local crafts, and the great encyclopaedias, and that great
series, the *Dictionary of National Biography*, which will
contain the life of anyone notable – saint, scientist, poet,
painter, explorer, inventor, novelist, soldier, high-
wayman, forger, murderer – who may have been born or
have lived where you live, or may lie underneath a brass

in the floor of your church or below some huge monument in twirls of marble.

In the secondhand bookshops not everything is going to be expensive. Persist. Poke about in corners. Climb the ladder, get your fingers filthy. Pull out old maps (often in neat green cases with a label) wedged half out of sight between the books.

If you find the book you want, the bookseller will have written the price inside. All the same, ask him the price. He may relent, and make it not quite so much after all. When you leave, ask him, too, if he has a catalogue. Take it home, and read it from cover to cover (it is usually printed on the covers). If he is demanding pounds for a book you do not very much want, he may be demanding only pennies for the next one, which you do want:

437. **STONEHENGE.** Jones (Inigo). The most noble Antiquity of Great Britain, vulgarly called Stoneheng, on Salisbury Plain, restor'd. Folio, contemporary calf gilt. £10/10/–. Magnificent copy. 1725.

438. **DEWPONDS.** Pugsley (Alfred J.). Dewponds in Fable and Fact. A collection and criticism of existing knowledge on these curiosities. Small 8vo. Poor copy. Stained. Scarce. 3/6. 1939.

Who cares about the stains?

All catalogues about things you like are pleasant to read, even if you do not buy much from them. And of all catalogues, ones about secondhand books (I think) are the best.

Bookshop or local library. But keep an eye as well on the shops which supply only new books, since they are likely to stock anything local which has just been published. Also see if the museum (sometimes the headquarters of the county's natural history and archaeological society, which may have its own library) does not publish and sell pamphlets about things you want to find – as well as exhibiting such things in the cases and collections.

If you turn to the end of some books, you will discover

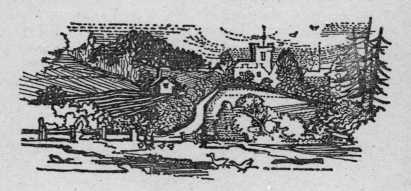

THE APPROACH TO SELBORNE

bibliographies, or book-lists, which tell the reader where still more information is to be had. You will see that the books mentioned are often divided into 'general' and 'particular'. Very well. I shall mention 'particular' books for each chapter, some to buy (or be given), some to read in libraries. But for this brief chapter which has nearly come to an end, I am going to recommend that you read (if you haven't read them already) two books for explorers and finders which are 'general', decidedly.

One is by Gilbert White: *The Natural History of Selborne*,** or in full, *The Natural History and Antiquities of Selborne in the County of Southampton*, first published in 1789, and reprinted, I should think, hundreds of times.

The other is *Walden; or, Life in the Woods*,** by Henry David Thoreau, also reprinted scores, if not hundreds, of times since it was first published in America in 1863.

You may never go to Selborne, which is still there (the 'County of Southampton' is Hampshire) and not spoilt; and you may never go to Walden Pond, which is in Massachusetts, and still there and quite considerably spoilt. It does not matter. It does not matter that these two books are quite a deal about natural history – unlike the book you are reading. I think you should read them both because they are two of the best encouragers and appetizers, two of the best books to encourage exploration. Gilbert White, in strong clear English, wrote about everything which tickled his mind from echoes, eels, toads, tortoises to forests, folklore, poisonous plants, fairy ring mushrooms, truffles, and Selborne church and why the Yew was planted in the churchyard.

As you read it, his book is one for picking and choosing, and jumping (there is no law compelling you to read all books right through, you might remember – including this book). ·

Also you may need to pick and skip a bit in *Walden*, which seemed to me when I read it first, a special box of delights like *Swiss Family Robinson* with the nonsense left out. Thoreau lived out in the woods by the green depths of Walden Pond, in a house he built for himself, with furniture he made for himself, existing rebelliously by the labour of his own hands. He wrote about sands, solitude, independence, bathing, birds, animals, snow, and the blue ice which formed across Walden Pond and then melted again into sparkling water in the spring.

Both these two you can buy in your secondhand book-shop. They should not be difficult to find or cost very much. My copy of *Walden* cost me 2½p, my *Natural History of Selborne* cost 37½p.

Exploration – or looking and finding – is another thing as well: it is a kind of long, personal poem, written, read, and enjoyed by the explorer. All poems in a way are records by imaginative explorers, so I am going to suggest that you read – some time before you finish this book – four poems you may not know; or that you read these four again if you do know them.

One is by Thomas Hardy (who liked seeing the stars reflected in a pool of water) – the poem called *After-wards*, about himself, stars and hedgehogs on the lawn, and a tolling bell.

One is *The Lyke-Wake Dirge* (no one knows who wrote it) which they used to sing in the North of England at wakes, when a body was waiting to be buried (a *lyke* is a dead man). The next one is *Ozymandias*, by Shelley; about one of the kings of Egypt. Shelley wrote it after he had seen a colossal head of Ozymandias which had just been transported from Egypt to the British Museum.

The fourth and last poem is the long one by Christopher Smart called *A Song to David*, in which there are scaléd mermaids, myrrh, cocoa, amber, humming-birds, swordfishes, lizards and lions, and whales:

> *Strong is the lion – like a coal*
> *His eyeball – like a bastion's mole*
> *His chest against the foes:*

> *Strong the gier-eagle on his sail,*
> *Strong against tide, th' enormous whale*
> *Emerges as he goes.*

I will tell you why, of all poems, I have suggested these four (which you will find in my anthology *The Cherry Tree*). Each of them seems to me an explorer's poem. Two of them suggest that the world is full of delights, which is true, two of them that you may turn the corner and find a mystery; and *The Lyke-Wake Dirge* and *Afterwards* and *Ozymandias* make us feel one of the strangest things of all – the passing of time, the passing of life.

Later on you will find a separate chapter about poems and poets, especially ones who had to do with your own neighbourhood. Meanwhile, recalling that I spoke of 'general' books and 'particular' books, I am going to suggest the first 'particular' book you should borrow or buy if you can: the book for your county in the Penguin series about the Buildings of England, edited by Nikolaus Pevsner. You may be unlucky, Nikolaus Pevsner may not have reached your county yet, though so far more than thirty of these books have been published.

He tells you which are the old – or new – buildings to look at, and why; about the churches in particular, or the castles, even about prehistoric camps and tombs. He tells you when they were built.

But he hasn't room to say much about their history – about who lived in these buildings or what they did, let's say, in the Civil War. So another of the first books worth buying for yourself is a guidebook.

If you can, buy one of *Murray's Hand-books for Travellers***, published county by county or several counties in one volume, in the last century, each with a map at the end in a pocket (be sure that the map is still there); each bound in bright red like a letter-box, and lettered in gold like this, end on:

Hand-book
For
Devon
7/6
London
John Murray

In some ways – so much has been discovered in the last hundred years – these red guidebooks will be out of date. But they will inform you, for instance, about local battlefields, about strange occurrences in your neighbourhood, about curious or great or good or beastly men, from saints to murderers, who may have lived in some place you know.

A secondhand bookshop will charge you anything from ten to fifty pence for a Murray hand-book, and about the same or a little more for one of Nikolaus Pevsner's books secondhand.

But do not forget the maps of our Chapter I. In many ways maps make a better guide even than guidebooks.

Some of the books mentioned in this chapter have stars against them. So will other books in other chapters. These are the ones you ought to find especially useful. Extra inexpensive ones are marked with two stars.

3

NAMES AND DATES.
ALSO PHOENIXES AND SALAMANDERS

SINCE exploring begins at home, do you know every-
ting about the house you live in? Or the house next
door? When was it built? If it is old, and made of stone,
or tiled with stones, where do you think the stones and
tiles were quarried? It might be worth looking and discovering; and discovering also what kind of stone was
used, among all the kinds from limestone to granite. If
the house is old and made of brick, where did they make
the bricks? Probably not so far off.

I asked those questions about our house, which is both
stone and brick; and had some fun out of the answers;
because the stone – a hard chalk – came from quarries in
the cliff behind the house, while the bricks came from a
place where I hadn't thought to find clay-pits and traces
of old kilns. My clue to the kilns was one of those original
Ordnance maps which I mentioned in the first chapter.
It marked brick kilns (the date of the map was 1828) five
miles away, right up on the high chalk downs, where the
wind blows and there are barrows and hefty sarsen
stones (also used for building houses) and wheatears nesting in the summer, and mushrooms in the short turf.

There were no buildings left. But under thorn trees
there were the dark pits where they dug the clay out of
beds or pockets of clay which are scattered here and
there in the chalk of the downs. Near the pits there was a

hard, flat, small field, with bits of brick among the grass. In corners we found a few old irregular bricks, which exactly matched some of the bricks in the house in size and in colour. They were stamped with the maker's initials.

We could imagine the kilns smoking against the blue sky, and whips cracking, and waggons rumbling away over the downs, loaded with new bricks; though perhaps the bricks were carried away to our house, not on waggons at all, but on string after string of pack-horses.

So even bricks had a story. Also since one thing leads to another, let me add that by looking for kilns we found a dewpond (dewponds are not filled with dew, but good honest rain), a bowl-barrow with an outer bank, a long barrow, several pounds of mushrooms, and a badger's earth in a slope of the downs, looking out over the world. The badgers there live deep inside the white chalk. In wet weather, when they come out they have wet, white feet, and they imprint a wet, white track down the green of the hill as if it had been traced out by a lawn marker.

Look round the house carefully and see if there are not inscriptions no one has noticed. Some inscriptions, though, may be obvious. If an architect built the house in the eighteenth century, he may have put a stone somewhere in front, in the front wall, carved with his name and the date. Or perhaps the first owner or first inhabitant was proud of the new house and put his name on a stone in the face of one of the chimneys.

It will be a poser, all the same, if you find only his initials. On the chimney of my house a very neat stone says just this and no more:

R S 1668

I did not know who R.S. was; but before he built the chimney he had carved his initials inside, in a still older part of the house. Some plaster fell off by the kitchen window and showed the lettering, this time with the S turned around:

R·Ƨ· 1625

Tantalizing, because R.S. was somebody – and somebody who walked around the house and looked out of the door and helped to wear hollows in the stones on the floor and sat in the kitchen and I suppose had a wife (perhaps she helped to trim his beard for him in the kitchen) and several children. Or perhaps R S 1625 was the father who built the first house before the Civil War began, and R S 1668 was the son, who added a new piece with a grander chimney two years after the Great Fire of London?

There are ways, though, of finding out – which will be entertaining to try, even if they do not succeed. If you have such a problem, your father or the landlord may have the old deeds of the house, on vellum (a deed being a sealed document containing the terms of an agreement to let the house, or sell it, or even to build it), which will be worth looking at, anyhow. There may be a clue to people who lived in your house in the registers in the church safe; the books in which, by law, the vicars or rectors for hundreds of years have entered the name of everyone baptized or married or buried. Registers again, like old deeds, give you a real flavour of time as you turn over the crinkly stained pages and read through them, and struggle, if they go back far enough, with earlier handwriting. Or there might be a clue in old accounts kept by the churchwardens. If they exist, these accounts

as well should be in the church safe; and they will tell
you much about life as it used to be lived.

Deeds, registers, churchwardens' accounts – here you
have only a beginning. Ask who knows about the old
documents of your neighbourhood. Ask at the museum.
Then tackle him. I doubt if he will bite, any more than
the librarian or the secondhand bookseller or the
museum people.

As I say, look round your house on the outside; but be
careful to do it also in the very early morning or early
evening. Somebody may have scratched his name with a
date somewhere on the wall, or carved it neatly but so

STONEHENGE: CARVINGS OF DAGGER AND AXE-HEAD

faintly that you can detect it now only when the light
strikes low across the wall and fills the letters of the inscription with shadow.

A scribble and a date of that kind tell you, at any rate,
that the house must have been built by that time. Indeed
faint carvings on the stones have just given an indication
of when the great mysterious Stonehenge was built.

At Stonehenge, first of all, a name led to seeing the

carvings. In the past many people have cut their names into the great pillars, or uprights, of Stonehenge (including Sir Christopher Wren, the architect who built St Paul's). On a summer evening in 1953, when the sunlight was just at the right revealing angle, an archaeologist was on the point of photographing one of these names which was carved slightly above eye-level on one of the two uprights of a trilithon, or triple-stone (two uprights with a third stone across the top).

The name was IOH: LVD: DEFERRE, perhaps the name of a French map-maker who would have cut it there about 1700, IOH standing for Johannis, Latin for John or Jean, and LVD for Ludovicus, the Latin for Louis.

The archaeologist was focusing his camera, when he noticed on his ground-glass screen two shapes on the rock below the name. He went over and looked; and made out a dagger and an axe-head.

The axe-head shape represents a kind of bronze axe made in Ireland between 1600 and 1400 B.C. The dagger shape represents, not exactly but near enough, a kind of bronze dagger made by the ancient Greeks in Mycenae about 1600 to 1500 B.C.

Thousands and thousands of visitors had been to Stonehenge, hundreds of archaeologists had examined Stonehenge inch by inch, and Johannis Ludovicus Deferre had carved his name letter by letter on that stone; and none of them – perhaps because they never looked at the right moment when the sun was striking across the surface – had noticed the dagger and the axe.

Soon after a boy ten years old found more axes on another stone.

Here I am going to add a postscript. A few pages back I mentioned those initials R.S. carved on the chimney of my house and carved again in the kitchen. I did find out about R.S. – by accident. A friend bought some documents, on vellum, in a saleroom in London, and he saw that one of these documents listed all the fields owned or rented by an R.S., who lived where? In my parish, and in my house. And he gave me this document for Christmas.

R.S. was Richard Spackman. Once I had that clue, things became easy. I knew the family I had to look for. I found that R.S. of 1625 by the kitchen window was the grandfather, and that R.S. of 1668 on the chimney slab was the grandson. I found that one Spackman from my house had become a remarkable carver and woodworker in the eighteenth century; and that another, at the time of the Civil War, had invented a musket with four barrels.

There are Spackmans still living in the neighbourhood, but they had forgotten that this house had belonged to their ancestors. Like his Civil War ancestor, one of them is an inventor in a small way. Odder still, I remembered that it was a Richard Spackman, a builder from our shopping town, who had added a new room for me to the house, to hold my books. Though he did not know it at the time, and I did not know it, he had actually been working for me on a house his own ancestors had built.

See what may come from a single piece of luck.

Postscript to a postscript: after all that, I wondered what a 'spackman' had been, and I discovered that the name had originally meant a 'speakman', or spokesman. For generations these Spackmans had been the leading family in my parish, which was always poor and remote. For generations they had been inventive and clever. Perhaps that was why one of them long ago in the Middle Ages had been called the Speakman – the man who was clever enough to speak for his neighbours, their 'speakman' perhaps to the Lord of the Manor or his bailiff.

Outside your house – and other houses – since we have been talking about outsides, look for a fire-mark.

To begin with, fire-marks were fixed to the wall by the Fire Offices, or fire insurance companies, which sprang up in the cities after everyone had been frightened by the Great Fire of London in 1666. The companies used to have their own fire-brigades, who knew by the marks which houses they had a duty towards in case of fire, their owners having paid a premium; in other words, a fee which guaranteed not only protection, but recompense if the house and the things inside it were destroyed.

All the same you might live miles from any fire-brigade. Even then, supposing you had made the proper arrangement with the Fire Officer, your house was still marked with a metal fire-mark as a guarantee and a reminder that it was insured.

The marks may be lead – these are early ones; or copper, or iron. They may be punched with the number of the 'policy,' the written agreement between the owner of the house and the Fire Office.

Each Fire Office had its own mark, with its own emblem. Outside your house, on the front, well out of reach from the ground, you may find the sun with a cheerful face – eyes, nose and mouth – and rays all around him, the Sun in his Splendour. This is still the fierce emblem of the Sun Insurance Office, which began in 1710.

Or the emblem may be a phoenix, waving its wings and rising new born from the flames, the emblem, this time, of another old Fire Office, the Phoenix Assurance

Company, which began in 1782. It was a suitable emblem, because the one phoenix in the world, according to legend, never died. It lived five hundred years, then flew with a load of spice to Heliopolis, the City of the Sun, in Egypt, and allowed itself to burn there in spice and flames, on top of an altar. From the spice and flames there came a worm, from the worm there came, or quickly grew, a freshly minted young phoenix, which flew off to India to begin another five hundred years of life.

The only trouble about fire-marks is that people have collected them, so there are not so many left on houses as there used to be. A pity, because once a fire-mark is removed no one can discover it for himself, and put a ladder up and examine it, and then busy himself with its history. Which reminds me of one other important fact I have already mentioned – that collecting is not only collecting things that can be removed and taken home. Memory is the best of all museums, and things of every kind can also be collected, first of all, into a notebook or a sketchbook.

Keeping a diary is collecting – making a collection of your impressions and your feelings and everything you need to remember. If you do not keep a diary every day (which I agree is a bothersome thing to do), keep a notebook for special days, special records. It is a good plan to have large notebooks at home, and fill them up from small notebooks or small sketchbooks which will go into a pocket. All the better if you can draw what you see or find, as well as describe it in words. On the beach of one of the desert islands of Scilly, at low tide, we found two large rusted guns out of a warship of sailing days. Two cannon cannot be carried home in the pocket. But we could draw them, and we did (less trouble than taking a camera). We sent a sketch to the National Maritime

Museum at Greenwich, and were told by the museum the age of the guns and what kind they were.

Whether you can draw or no, keep your records, your collections of the mind, in notebooks *which have plain paper*. It is more civilized. Lines suggest that you do not know how to write; they also suggest class-rooms and exercise books. I know plain paper books are not to be had in every shop. They can always be bought in university towns. In London, if you are ever near the Law Courts, you can buy big plain paper books very cheap, of the kind barristers use for preparing their cases and their speeches (I get them for writing books in). Or go to shops where they sell artists' materials and buy sketchbooks – not the long kind with thick paper, but the ones which are bound and shaped like an exercise book, with plain paper of ordinary thickness.

This chapter is lengthening; but I have not quite finished yet with walls and stones and with inscriptions of many kinds which are exciting to find and curious to read and sometimes worth collecting into notebooks and sketchbooks and sketches. Everywhere there are odd inscriptions about, set up because somebody, at some time, wanted something – probably himself – to be remembered or known.

It is a very old habit, as old as writing. Upstairs in the British Museum a little white stone statue of a king, with black eyebrows and black eyes, sits and stares at all the people going by, who do not look at him as they should. He is thirty-five centuries old, his name is Idrimi, and his father's name was Ilimilimma, and he was king of Alalakh in Syria. An inscription in Akkadian all over him, from his face to his feet, tells who he was and the gods he served and the battles he fought, and ends by threatening and cursing anyone who should damage

him. For all that, invaders came after a thousand years
and knocked him off a throne with lions carved on either
side, and tipped him broken into a pit; from which he
emerged when Alalakh was excavated by Sir Leonard
Woolley.

Forgotten kings and chiefs have left stones with their
names on them ten centuries old in our own country,
though – unfortunately – they never have as much to say
as Idrimi.

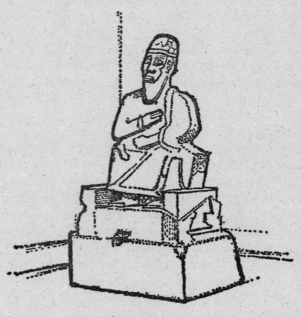

KING IDRIMI

But do not despise quite modern inscriptions. Stop
and read them and remember them, and copy them out,
when they are worth it, for what might be called your
CORPUS INSCRIPTIONUM BRITANNICORUM, or Collection

of British Inscriptions. There are plenty of them. On Salisbury Plain I know a memorial at one lonely place inscribed with details about a robbery there in 1839:

AT THIS SPOT

Mr. DEAN, of Imber, was Attacked and Robbed by Four Highwaymen, in the evening of Octr 21st 1839. After a spirited pursuit of three hours, one of the Felons BENJAMIN COLCLOUGH fell dead on Chitterne Down. THOMAS SAUNDERS, GEORGE WATERS & RICHARD HARRIS were eventually Captured and were convicted at the Ensuing Quarter Sessions at Devizes, and Transported for the term of Fifteen Years. This Monument is erected by Public Subscription as a warning to those who presumptuously think to escape the punishment God has threatened against
THIEVES and ROBBERS

Another memorial by the road near Stonehenge records the death of one of the first aviators, when his plane crashed.

You never know what you will come across. I was exploring once in Essex, along the estuaries, looking for 'red hills,' which are low mounds of red earth and of debris (often vitrified, or fused, and beautifully green) where more than two thousand years ago they made salt out of seawater which they ladled on to hot bars of earthenware. I knew there should be red hills near Little Wigborough, which, so far as any village goes, is only a pink farmhouse and a few trees and a small, squat, square-towered church set down by themselves on a low hill above a huge landscape.

I found the red hills. What I did not expect was a brass tablet saying that the tower of the church had been rebuilt after falling in an earthquake on April 22nd,

1884. Below a gravestone lay on the grass, broken in bits at the same time by the fall of the tower.

Afterwards I had to inform myself about the earthquake – not so difficult, because to my surprise there existed that book I have mentioned which gives the history of all the earthquakes of England (more of them than you would think).

Inscriptions are thickest of all in towns. In London especially an open eye will always encounter inscriptions odd and unexpected. My London favourite is a small brass plate in the floor of the bandstand under the green roof of trees in Lincoln's Inn Fields – so small that I do not suppose it is ever noticed by the girls who come there every day to play netball. It says in a very quiet voice, in a whisper, that just there, upon that spot, Lord William Russell was beheaded on July 21st, 1683.

Or in the churchyard of St Giles-in-the-Fields, near Tottenham Court Road. There without much trouble you can identify a sooty tomb-chest inscribed with a poem about 'Unparallel'd Penderel through the universe'. It is the grave of Richard Penderel, who helped Charles the Second to escape to France after the battle of Worcester in 1651.

Till lately Unparallel'd Penderel's descendants received a pension for his good services to the King of England.

This chapter has mentioned one or two special things as well as names, dates, and inscriptions.

Fire-marks: they have a book to themselves, Bertram Williams, 'Specimens of British Fire-marks',* 1934.

At the end of the chapter I spoke of English earthquakes and of exploring London. An old (not a modern) edition of Baedeker's 'Handbook to London',* say of

1923, *does not miss very much (it mentions the brass tablet about the cutting off of the head of Lord John Russell, for example). Easy to buy secondhand.*

If you want to know about earthquakes — ones in Great Britain since history began — the book is 'British Earthquakes', by C. Davison (1924).

4

YEW TREES, GREEN MEN,
AND MUCH ELSE

WITH UNPARALLEL'D PENDEREL we have come so close to church that churches may as well have this next chapter.

> GOOD FREND FOR IESVS SAKE FORBEARE,
> TO DIGG THE DVST ENCLOASED HEARE:
> BLEST BE Y MAN Y SPARES TIES STONES
> AND CVRST BE HE Y MOVES MY BONES

No prize is offered for telling me where that inscription is, and whose bones and stones are not to be disturbed, like Idrimi's statue.

The bones are Shakespeare's (who died in 1616, when he was fifty-two years old), the church is at Stratford-on-Avon. Shakespeare's bones never have been disturbed (though what if the manuscripts of *Hamlet* and *Macbeth* lay in his coffin?); and they are buried in the chancel, in front of the altar. On the wall above is a carved and coloured face of Shakespeare.

Don't you agree it is something to be able to walk into Stratford church and look down on this stone or 'ledger', overlying and guarding the dust and bones of the greatest poet of the world? Still, no one needs to have been Shakespeare for his monument to be something worth standing in front of and reading.

Which is one reason for this chapter about churches – or at any rate about a few things, monuments included, inside and outside.

It is *not* a chapter about Norman Early English and Decorated and Perpendicular and different kinds of arch and window in different centuries (look at the end of the chapter for a book which describes the styles of churches and almost everything they contain). Your own church, all the same, is likely to be the one really old building you know well; and in villages the church always is the first building to make for.

Outside. Though it will not be so old as the church itself, a very old yew tree rooting into the churchyard is a reminder that the church may have been built where men worshipped strange gods before the first missionaries ever landed in England.

Trees and tall stones were sacred. They could be gods. A tree rooted in the ground or a tall stone set upright is roughly man-shaped – or god-shaped, if you think of a god in the shape of a man or a woman.

About A.D. 550 or 560, Samson, a holy man from Wales, was riding across Cornwall on his way to Brittany when he saw men worshipping an abominable image in a high place – an upright stone of the kind we now call a 'menhir' (which is the Breton for 'long stone').

He persuaded them to stop, and took a piece of iron and carved a cross on the stone.

In Corsica there are sacred places, lately found and cleared, which are more than three thousand years old, and which are peopled by menhirs with faces carved on them; and if ever you go to Rudston in the East Riding, be sure to visit the huge menhir still standing in the churchyard, towering up for 25 feet 6 inches, more than a foot taller than the tallest stone at Stonehenge. I think it was another 'abominable image'. But then the shrine became Christian, and a church was built there; and the English – the Anglo-Saxons – called that menhir the 'rood stone', the stone of the rood or cross of Christ. So the whole village is still 'Rudston(e)'.

If you like, the Rood Stone of Rudston is a stone tree; and a big tree in the churchyard, a big yew tree, is a living stone. Trees were worshipped. When the Englishman, St Boniface (who came from Devonshire), travelled to convert the Germans in their black forests, he came in 723 to Geismar and found the Germans worshipping a great oak tree of their god Wotan. He cut it down and used the timber to build a chapel to St Peter.

People used to ask why yew trees had been planted in churchyards. They forgot that trees had once been worshipped, and thought the reason might have been to supply yew for making bows. But to make yew bows it is necessary to fell the *whole tree* and then cut staves out of the trunk.

No, when you come across a yew tree among the tombstones and graves, remember that trees could be sacred, especially such trees as oak and yew, which grow big and endure for centuries. Remember that yew trees – or yew leaves – are poisonous and powerful; that the most ancient wooden weapon ever found – a spear from Clacton-on-Sea in Essex, some seventy thousand years old – was made of yew.

Pagans became Christians; instead of cutting down the old sacred yews they allowed them to remain alongside Christian churches. Then when the yews died, by habit yews were planted again, and so it continued long after everybody had forgotten the ancient whys and wherefores.

But people found a new why and wherefore. On Palm Sunday they wanted green leaves to bring to mind

Christ's entry into Jerusalem, when the people had cut palm branches and strewn them in the way. Palm Sunday, though, comes next before Easter, when spring has hardly started the new leaves growing. So leaves for the Palm Sunday procession were cut off the evergreen churchyard yew.

We still plant yews in the churchyard – at any rate yews like bushes, of the form which is called 'fastigiate,' and is like a bundle of upright branches. All these fastigiate yews descend from a single tree found at Powerscourt in Ireland.

Outside, around the yew, the gravestones are worth peering at for their cherubs and flowers and skulls and hour glasses and inscriptions and dates – which is the oldest one in the churchyard? – but I am going to keep memorials till we get inside the church.

Outside we still have one matter to look into – or up to.

Can you answer a riddle?

> *I puff my breast out, my neck swells*
> *I have a head, I have a tail held high,*
> *One foot and eyes and ears,*
> *A back; my beak is hard.*
> *My neck is high, I have two sides,*
> *And a rod is in my middle.*
> *I have a home above men,*
> *I put up with wretchedness*
> *When the tree-mover moves me.*
> *Rain, in my situation, beats me*
> *Hail hits at me, hoar-frost clothes me,*
> *Cold snow sits on me, pierced in my belly.*

That is a riddle the old Englishmen – the Anglo-Saxons – asked each other, about A.D. 750.

Look up and you may see the answer, a true weather-cock gilded and glittering in the sun.

There is something to know about weathercocks. They are useful – that is obvious – telling at a glance if the wind has changed, if it has veered round, for example, from east and a clear sky to south-west with cloud and a likelihood of rain; and I think there are three reasons why a bird – and a rooster – was chosen.

First, it was noticed that a bird always perches to wind (so that its feathers are not ruffled). A bird is a natural weathercock.

Second, to point into the wind, there must always be more wind-catching surface at the tail end. So a rooster, with so large an up-and-down tail, is just the bird. No use having a magpie, or a goose, or an owl.

Third, the weathercock surmounts the church. And a rooster, which crows early in the morning, stands high above the church to suggest watch and pray and wake-fulness against sin. The crowing of the cock reminded St Peter of his denial of Christ.

Last of all, perhaps most important of all, is some-thing else we have forgotten – that the cock was thought to be a very powerful bird, which protected houses and shooed away evil spirits. In *Hamlet* Marcellus reported that the ghost of Hamlet's murdered father faded on the crowing of the cock. 'Some say', Marcellus added about the power of the cock,

> *that ever 'gainst that season comes*
> *Wherein our Saviour's birth is celebrated,*
> *The bird of dawning singeth all night long:*
> *And then, they say, no spirit dare stir abroad;*
> *The nights are wholesome; then no planets*
> * strike.*

So why not have a bird of dawning permanently above

your house or above the church? Bright and gilded, it was always on duty against evil. Up there on the church the weathercock was always protecting the village.

Some of the best and oldest weathercocks are rounded and hollow instead of flat. One weathercock, set up in the Middle Ages above the church of Ottery St Mary in Devon, actually crows, or makes a noise at least, against evil spirits. Or rather the wind, when it is sufficiently strong, makes a noise through tubes in its body.

WEATHERVANE OF 1661, OXBOROUGH, NORFOLK

Keep a look out – or up – and now and again you may also see a weather-fish on a church instead of a weather-cock, set there because a fish is the symbol of Christ. The church at Piddinghoe in Sussex carries a rounded weather-fish – a sea-trout, to be exact, since sea-trout were netted in the river below.

More ordinary weathervanes show an arrow and a metal flag. These are proper 'vanes', vane coming – I hope you like words – from *fana*, the Old English word for a flag. The metal flag is often a pennon with a divided tail such as knights in the Middle Ages carried on their lances, each one blazoned with their arms.

It seems odd (to us) to have buried people in churches; though it is less odd than burying them under the floor of the cave you lived in, and went on living in, which was a habit in the Old Stone Age. In the olden days it was the poor who were buried outside in the churchyard, and the better off, until there was no more room, who were buried inside, in greater holiness, out of the rain.

And the better off you were among these better off, the nearer your burial place was to the altar.

Shakespeare was rich when he died at Stratford in 1616, so he found a place inside the altar rails, in the chancel, the holiest part of the church; the part which in the Middle Ages, at any rate, they believed to be filled with the presence of God.

As well as the rich, though, priests were often buried in front of the altar, where they had served so regularly in their lifetime.

Don't be snobbish about monuments or about mere *oldness*. It used to be felt that nothing was really old (monuments included) or worth a glance, if it was not medieval, or if it did not belong, at the latest, to the age of Shakespeare and Queen Elizabeth. The rule is to make no rules. Allow yourself to be interested by everything you find interesting. I like to read the poems on the tombs and the tricks and fancies, the anagrams on the dead man's name, the acrostics, all of which belong very much to Elizabethan and Jacobean times; and then (more and more common after about 1660) the recital of all his good deeds and virtues, as if he wished to tell them all to St Peter when he arrived at the door of Heaven.

You soon discover that people buried as near as their wills or their heirs could get them to the altar, were often not at all modest. In the Middle Ages monuments were fairly quiet, an effigy on a stone chest, hands together in prayer, or an engraved brass on the floor. Then they get bigger and bigger, taller and taller. But they can still be

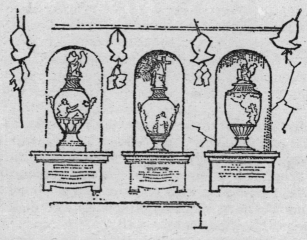

HAREFIELD, MIDDLESEX: URNS TO THE THREE LADIES
NEWDIGATE, 1774, BY RICHARD HAYWARD AND
JOHN BACON

intriguing, and beautiful at times, though they shout with such a loud voice. I like two monuments I know, one in Yorkshire, one in Gloucestershire. The Yorkshire monument in Calverley church recites the virtues of Sir

Walter Calverley, who died in 1749, in no less than seventy-one lines.

'He possessed,' his memorial boasts, 'every qualification which distinguishes the great man, he cultivated every virtue which adorns the good one'. And when he reached his eightieth year 'Death by an easie, gradual dissolution, opened to him a glorious immortality'. I wondered why the monument boasted so much.

My Gloucestershire memorial, at Tetbury, put up nearly a hundred years later, is quite another story. Modesty has come back:

> In a Vault underneath
> lie several of the Saunderses,
> late of this parish: particulars
> the Last Day will disclose.
>
> AMEN

There is no end to the things which can be learnt from monuments. Hauberks and helmets and sabbatons and bainbergs, swords and daggers, clothes, from liripipes and houppelandes and cover-chefs and cotehardies to ruffs and doublets, from the swaddling clothes tight around a baby to rich coats and waistcoats under vast periwigs – churches have them all.

You can discover what men thought about death and resurrection. You can see Death dancing as a skeleton, you can see emblems of mortality, a boy blowing bubbles, Time and Life trickling away in one of those hourglasses we only use now (though we are just as mortal in the long run) for timing eggs on the boil, or Time like an old bent man carrying the scythe which cuts us all down like flowers in the grass. 'Man that is born of woman hath but a short time to live, and is full of misery. He cometh up, and is cut down, like a flower.' Figures of abbots and bishops sometimes lie on their tomb-chests as cadavers, or corpses, covered with toads and those wiggling corpse worms which do not really exist. Knights in armour may rest their pointed stone feet on a stone dog. Sometimes in the Bronze Age the dead were buried in barrows with a dog at their feet to help them to hunt in the next world.

A monument inside or a gravestone outside may be decorated with the tools of a man's fame or trade, much as in ancient times his actual tools or weapons might be buried with him. In a Wiltshire church a great archaeologist has on his memorial a theodolite and picks and spades and skulls. A carpenter who made a great fortune in London stands splendidly in marble, in another Wiltshire church, with his marble tools in a marble bag by his feet. Out in the churchyard at Wiveton in Norfolk a stone to Thomas Smith, millwright, who died in 1725, is carved with the tools he used in windmills and watermills, his dividers, his saw, his axe, his mill bill and his 'thrift', which was a tool for sharpening the millstones which ground the corn into flour.

Look in the *Dictionary of National Biography* or a large county history in the library to see if there is any account of the men so grandly commemorated near the altar. I looked up that Sir Walter Calverley. Though I did not find him, I did find his ancestor, another Walter Calverley, who had been one of the most famous of all murderers. He killed his wife and two sons, in 1605, then was tortured to death by what was called the *peine forte et dure*, the hard and powerful torture, which was having weights heaped on one's back.

It was that skeleton in the family cupboard, I suspect, which caused all his descendant's virtues to be so magnified in seventy-one lines of epitaph.

Search, too, in corners of the big curly intricate monuments and the big smooth flattish monuments of white marble and you will often find the names of the sculptors who made them – Epiphanius Evesham or Peter Scheemakers or John Bacon, Joseph Wilton, Joseph Nollekens, John Flaxman, Henry Behnes, Richard Westmacott.

Joseph Wilton fect., the signature may read, Joseph Wilton *fecit*, or made it, or *Joseph Wilton inven. et fect.*, he invented this, or designed this, and made it.

By the way, the faces which look so severe, or so strong, or so noble, or so gentle on medieval effigies of lords and knights and their ladies and bishops and abbots will not usually have been likenesses. The carvers at their stone quarry had no portraits to guide them. They simply made a figure which would be young or old, man or woman, according to instructions, and of a dignity and in clothes or armour proper to the dead person's rank.

In the seventeenth century and afterwards rich men and their ladies would have had their likenesses drawn or painted. A life mask might have been made of them, or a death mask before they were put into their coffins. The sculptor, intent by now on a likeness, would have drawing or painting or mask to guide him as he chipped and smoothed his white marble.

I have often spoken of 'emblems' or 'symbols'. They are tokens, easily and quickly understood, standing for something else, perhaps something thought, something imagined, which is not so easy to explain, or would need the use of too many words.

We are always using emblems and symbols, often in rather a practical, dull way – for example, the green light which says Go, and the red light which says Stop, or the coloured pole announcing a barber. In the Middle Ages they loved symbols, partly because few people could read, still more because everything seemed to have its meaning in the scheme of God and Heaven and Hell. So churches are full of carved symbols, on capitals, ceilings, the ends of benches, the sides of the font, and everywhere.

Just as the weathercock outside says watch and pray, as well as the direction of the wind, so birds and beasts carved inside the church often have their message.

The Dove stands for the Holy Ghost. The Lamb of God holding the Cross (another symbol) with one foot stands for Christ. So does a kneeling camel, which is Christ taking on himself the load of the sins of the world.

The Devil has many shapes in church carvings. He is a dragon (a serpent with wings), he is a crocodile, because crocodiles live a double life in water and on land, he is a fox, because by legend the fox lay down and shammed dead and ate the birds which flew down to eat the fox, just as the cunning Devil tries to deceive and capture and devour the souls of Christians.

In churches you have the winged lion for St Mark (look up the *Book of Revelations* IV.7 and *Ezekiel* I.4–10 for the beasts which were taken to mean the Evangelists), the eagle – as on lecterns, holding up the Bible with its wings – for St John; and a winged bull for St Luke.

There are good creatures and bad in church. The lion is usually good, so is the hart; both of them fight the dragon of evil (the hart more often fights evil in the shape of a snake, though it panted after the water brooks (Psalm 42), according to medieval notions, because it was so heated by the flaming breath of dragons). Squirrels are carved sometimes, because according to legend they could cross streams on a leaf or a piece of wood. So they symbolize crossing the dangerous sea of life on the Cross of Christ. Legend makes the pelican peck at its own breast (as you see it in the carvings) and feed the small pelicans on its blood. A man in the Middle Ages when he looked up and saw a pelican on a corbel (which is a stone bracket) of his new glistening parish church, would know at once that it stood for Christ loving his Church. The pelican shed its blood for its nestlings, Christ shed his blood for men.

Wild boars, when they are carved, stand for wickedness and cruelty, like the wickedness and cruelty of princes. Frogs stand for horrible sinners. Owls are reminders of sin and foolishness, choosing night instead of

CARVED BLEMYAE AND THRESHERS

day. Sometimes they are carved alone, sometimes the owl in the carving is mobbed by smaller birds; which are the righteous jeering at the sinner.

In churches I like to find some of the semi-human creatures that never were – especially the Blemya and the Wodewose and the Mermaid. I do not know what the Blemya symbolized. But he is a man with legs and no head, and with eyes, nose, and mouth in his stomach; or you could describe him as a stomach on legs. Perhaps he is Greed or Gluttony.

Wodewoses are wild hairy men of the woods, the origin of the idea of wolf children, like Mowgli in *The Jungle Book*. Mermaids are sirens, like the ones which sang to Ulysses and would have lured him to death if he had not made his men tie him to the mast. They are evil, of course, and are carved as a symbol of temptation by wicked pleasures.

Blemyae, wodewoses, and mermaids are not so very common. Easier to discover is the mysterious Green Man, or Jack-in-the-Green, or Man-in-the-Oak. You can recognize him by the leaves and branches all round his face, usually oak or may (which were magical trees). The branches grow out of his mouth; and as a rule the Green Man frowns and looks sad or half-dead. Not surprising, because he is the May King. On May Day, in the village plays and ceremonies, he was sacrificed, dying for all the death of the plants in winter, his May Queen weeping by his side. Then he jumped up to life again, a symbol in his fresh green garland of oak leaves or may leaves of the new spring and the new leaves and flowers and crops and life; and he now danced and danced in delight with his May Queen.

That explains why the branches, with all their leaves, grow out of his mouth, usually one branch on each side, life out of death.

This same Green Man used to walk at the head of May Day processions in London, with fireworks exploding out of his green leaves, and he has given his name to hundreds of inns.

It may seem strange that he should be in church so often, but I think he was allowed there as a symbol of Christ's resurrection out of death.

Look for him among his leaves on bosses in the ceiling, on stone brackets outside and inside the church, and wherever there are carved decorations. Green Men can be very high up in the great churches and cathedrals. So in hunting for them, and making out their details, it helps if you have a pair of field-glasses; which can be used, as well, for making out the wonderful details of old stained glass, fifty or sixty feet above your head. Field-glasses, in fact, are not only for watching birds or for searching distant views.

GREEN MAN, COVENTRY

*Even weathercocks have a small book to themselves, 'English Weathervanes', by A. Needham (1953).***

About animals in church (and much else) you will find all you need in two books by Miss M. D. Anderson, who has travelled all over England exploring churches,

*'Animal Carvings in British Churches' (1938)**

*'The Imagery of British Churches' (1955)**

*Also by Miss Anderson, you will enjoy 'Looking for History in British Churches' (1951).***

About monuments, here are three books you should find in the public library, 'English Church Monuments', by F. H. Crossley (1921), 'English Church Monuments, 1510–1840', by Katherine Esdaile (1946); and to follow up the signatures on the later monuments, 'A Dictionary of British Sculptors', by Rupert Gunnis (1953).

For the clothes they wear on the old monuments look

at 'Handbook of English Medieval Costume', by C. W. and P. Cunnington (1952);* and 'A History of English Costume', by Iris Brooke (1946).*

Last, two books altogether about old churches, 'The English Mediaeval Parish Church', by G. H. Cook (1954, 1969); and 'How to Study an Old Church', by A. Needham (1944).

5

CHURCHES AND SAINTS

CHURCHES are usually dedicated to saints. We take saints rather for granted, as if, for example, a St Catherine's church somewhere was no more than a name distinguishing it from a St Michael's church somewhere else. But if you ask about saints, beginning with the one your local church is dedicated to, you have a chance of learning many curious and unexpected things about the Dark Ages and the Middle Ages, and many curious legends.

First of all, what is a saint? Saints are the holy men of a religion (it isn't only Christians, of course, who remember their holy men with special affection. Buddhists and Confucians, to think of two more of the great religions of the world, have their 'saints', even if they don't, like Christians, put an St in front of their names). But then 'holy' is another word we use rather too easily.

A saint, in our tradition, is someone who was good, who lived a specially good life, and so was thought to be enjoying life in heaven after his death. Often his death was violent: he was told to give up believing in a new (and kinder and gentler) god: he refused: and then in times which were even more cruel than our own, he was tortured by kings, princes, noblemen and so on, who were afraid that this new Christian belief would bring down the anger of the old gods they believed in. The good man – in spite of his goodness – would be tortured and killed: then he was looked upon, not only as a saint, but as a 'martyr' as well, a martyr meaning originally (in Greek) a witness.

Saints and martyrs. If you could have asked somebody alive in the fifteenth century – let us say a wool merchant in the Cotswolds or a clothier, i.e. a cloth merchant, in Norfolk or Suffolk or Wiltshire – what saints and martyrs were, he would have replied: 'They are blessed people in heaven, and if I pay respect to them and pray to them, they will intercede with God for me, and then perhaps the bad things which I have done will be pardoned, and I shall have a chance of going to heaven as well'.

If you asked 'How do you know who the saints and martyrs are?', he might have said, 'Well, wonderful things happened where they died, or by their graves; and our priests read out their legends, their stories, and tell us all about them' (a 'legend' originally meaning something that is read out, and then a collection of the lives of saints).

Thinking you were a strange – and perhaps dangerous – person to be so ignorant about saints and martyrs, the clothier or wool merchant might have gone on to explain that everyone needed the help of saints, that everyone needed a 'Christian name', the same of a saint likely to help him; and that all sorts of callings had their own special saints, specially interested, let us say, in cobblers, or carpenters or shoeing smiths, or wool-combers, or huntsmen or sailors, because in life these saints had some connection with such trades or callings.

He might have added that of course there were other saints venerated by everyone, St Mary the Queen of Heaven—

Blessed Mary, mother virginal,
Integrate maiden, star of the sea,
Have remembrance at the day final
On thy poore servant now praying to thee—

and the archangels, also thought of as saints, St Michael,
St Gabriel, St Raphael—

Holy archangel Michael,
Saint Gabriel and Raphael,
Ye bring me to the Castel
Where all souls fare well

— especially St Michael, the captain of the heavenly
host, the provost of Heaven, who would weigh the souls
of the dead, in his scales, at the Last Judgment.

The medieval merchant might have told you to walk
up to the church, in white stone, which he had just rebuilt with his own money, from bales of wool or rolls of
serge, and look at the new painting of St Christopher, on
the wall, just opposite the south door — St Christopher,
the ferryman, carrying the child Christ on his shoulder
over a river or a dangerous estuary. St Christopher
interceded in heaven for travellers, since there was much
danger in travel, especially in the Middle Ages; and if in
the morning you paid your respects to huge St Christopher on the wall, through the south door, it was held
that you would be safe from harm all day.

Your rich wool merchant, your clothier, might have
boasted too, that he and his friends had been able to buy
a relic, an actual piece of the body, of the patron saint
of the church, for which a clever goldsmith in London
or Canterbury or Exeter or York had made them a
shrine.

Of course the church might have relics of other saints
as well, to strengthen the holiness of the building. There

would be chapels and altars in the church dedicated to other saints – if it was a church of any size. Saints, other than St Christopher, might be pictured on the walls, or in the bright glass of the windows, or on panels of a screen; or they might be carved around the church in stone or wood, in the bosses on the ceiling, perhaps, or on oak bench-ends. Round them might be carved or painted the signs or emblems by which they were known (remember, in the last chapter, how a lion with wings is the sign or emblem of St Mark, how the lectern eagle is the emblem of St John, and a winged bull the emblem of St Luke). Or the emblems, often something to do with their lives, may be painted or carved by themselves, without an actual likeness of the saint.

Of course in the Protestant reforms in England, Scotland and Wales at the end of the Middle Ages, praying to the saints was forbidden, shrines containing the relics of saints were broken up and the relics thrown away, pictures on church walls were covered with whitewash, statues and windows in coloured glass were broken, and bright saints came tinkling to the church floor.

An example I like to think about is St Catherine. Suppose St Catherine's name was given long ago in the Middle Ages to the church in your parish, or suppose she was given a chapel and an altar inside the church, then somewhere in the church you may still find her Catherine Wheel, her emblem – the object which was at the heart of the story of St Catherine's sainthood and martyrdom.

It was a story everybody knew, in all the countries of Europe. Let us see how it was told in the *Legenda Aurea, The Golden Legend,* the golden collection of stories about the saints, which was compiled by Jacobus de Voragine, a learned friar and bishop in Italy, seven hundred years ago.

Catherine was a beautiful young queen, who 'drank plentiously of the well of wisdom'. She lived in a palace in Alexandria, and was baptized by a hermit. Many of her subjects became Christians. Then there arrived in Alexandria one day her overlord, the Roman emperor Maxentius, determined to make all the people of Alexandria sacrifice to idols, and to kill all those who refused. Queen Catherine, eighteen years old and unmarried, disputed with the Emperor, who was so much affected by her learning that he sent for fifty philosophers to argue against her. She bettered them in argument, and they told the Emperor they would now be converted.

The Emperor had them burnt, all fifty.

Then he asked Catherine to marry him, and said that if she did, her image would be set up in Alexandria as a goddess. She said no. And the Emperor ordered her to be stripped and beaten with scorpions, and starved for 12 days in a dark prison. A white dove brought her food. She argued again with Maxentius. Maxentius again asked her to marry him, and ordered her to sacrifice to idols. No. In fury he said:

'Of these two choose thee one, or do sacrifice and live, or suffer divers torments and perish.'

'Tarry not to do what torments thou wilt,' said Catherine.

'And then a master warned and advised the king that he should make four wheels of iron, environed with sharp razors, cutting so that she might be horribly all de-trenched, and cut in that torment. ... And then was ordained that two wheels should turn against the other two by great force, so that they should break all that should be between the wheels.'

So here were the first Catherine Wheels. They failed to detrench her horribly, for 'Then the blessed virgin

prayed our Lord that he would break these engines to
the praising of his name, and for to convert the people
that were there. And anon as this blessed virgin was set
in this torment the angel of our Lord broke the wheels by
so great force that it slew four thousand paynims.'

The Emperor became even more mad and angry,
and ordered his men to cut off her head.

The unexpected result was something, like the Catherine Wheel, which medieval people always remembered when they thought of St Catherine: beheaded she
was, and 'there issued out of her body milk instead of
blood'.

When someone wrote a poem in 1430 asking the saints
to protect the King of England in his expedition to
France, St Catherine was one he included, and he remembered the milk:

> *Dere spouse of God, holy seynte Kateryne,*
> *Whose stedfast love myght change for no torment*
> *Nor faire promise, martyre and pure virgine,*
> *I beseche you to faveur myn entent;*
> *And lyke as mylke oute of your feyre nek went*
> *In stede of blode uppon your dying day,*
> *Hear my prayer and be with me alwey.*

The Golden Legend finished by saying that angels took
St Catherine's body 'and bare it unto the Mount of
Sinai, and buried it there honourably, and continually
oil runneth out of her bones which healeth all maladies
and sicknesses'. (Under Sinai there is still a monastery of
St Catherine.)

If you look for saints in churches, there you have the
kind of legend you may arrive at – this legend of the
Catherine to whom all Catherines or Katherines owe
their Christian name, whether they realize it or not;

and to whom all of us owe the Catherine Wheel on November 5th.

I think, by the way, that in calling the firework a Catherine Wheel, people were not commemorating the saint as much as remembering inn signs which were often painted with a likeness of St Catherine's bladed wheel. Inns were often called the Cat and Wheel or the Catherine Wheel, just as other inns were named the George and Dragon (St George killing the dragon of evil), or the Lamb and Flag (the Angus Dei, the Lamb of God, emblem of Christ). It seems a bit odd that emblems of saints, emblems of religion, gave their names to buildings where people went to drink and certainly not to pray. But there it was, they did.

Of course, people – Catholic and Protestant – grew more and more critical about saintly legend. St Catherine always reminds me of this because of a story told about a small Wiltshire village called Winterbourne Bassett which is near my home, and which has an old church of St Catherine.

It was remote and people did not change their ideas in Winterbourne Bassett as quickly as they did in London. The village had an old parish clerk, Simon Brunsdon, about the time of Shakespeare's death (which I don't need to tell you was in 1616). The Reformation, the Armada, Queen Elizabeth – they had all come and gone, all the saints had been hidden away under coats of whitewash for more than seventy years, but Simon Brunsdon was still St Catherine's man. 'When the Gadflye had happened to sting his Oxen, or Cowes, he would run after them, crying out, praying Good St Katherine of Winterbourne stay my Oxen, etc. This old Brunsdon was wont in the summer-time to leave his Oxen in the field, and goe to the church to pray to St Katherine.'

To John Aubrey, gossip and collector of scraps of

antiquity, who wrote that story down in 1688, it must
have seemed that the Middle Ages had gone on living in
Winterbourne Bassett, and in the parish clerk, long after
they had been dead everywhere else. Protestants and
Catholics too had begun sifting fancy from fact, legend
from history, impossible from possible; and this caused
havoc among saints.

People who write about saints today are doubtful, for
instance, if there ever was a St Catherine of Alexandria;
or if at any time there ever was a St Christopher acting
as a virtuous ferryman. Today they do not accept the
stories of St Christopher, which are told in *The Golden
Legend* and elsewhere, and which were believed by
everybody centuries ago – that he was a Canaanitish
giant, 12 cubits tall, an ogre, before he became a holy
man, before he was roasted, yet unharmed, on an iron
settle, and shot at by forty knights with arrows which
'hung in the air about, nigh him, without touching' –
except for one arrow which turned round and hit the eye
of the wicked pagan king who was torturing him. And so
on.

But I cannot see that much harm was done by such
stories, repeated in a simpler time than ours. There was
much poetry in them, as you will find if you pursue the
saints you encounter back into their legends.

Some of the other saints you are certain to come
across, if you look for dedications, or look in churches for
actual carvings and scraps of stained glass and paint-
ings, are

Saint Margaret of Antioch, leading a dragon on a
chain. Legend – she belongs more to legend than history
– says that this beautiful Christian girl of the third century was looking after sheep with her nurse and other
girls one day, when the provost or governor Olybrius

came by, and fell in love with her; but was horrified to
discover she was a Christian. She was tortured and imprisoned, to make her acknowledge the old gods. In
prison a demon appeared to her, who said his name was
Veltis, and that he was one of the demons whom Solomon had enclosed in a vessel of brass, which was broken
open, after Solomon's death, by the Babylonians. Later
a horrible dragon blustered into her prison – the Devil
himself – and was subdued when Margaret made the
sign of the cross. So she leads her dragon.

The Golden Legend adds an extra story that Margaret was swallowed by the dragon, whose belly broke
asunder, Margaret stepping out unharmed.

More than 200 of our old churches have St Margaret
for patron.

SAINT LAURENCE, martyred in Rome by the Emperor
Decius, who had him roasted on a gridiron, in A.D. 258,
so he is usually shown with a gridiron in one hand. According to *The Golden Legend,* he said to one of his per-
secutors, as he grilled, 'Learn, thou cursed wretch, that
thy coals give to me refreshing of coldness'. Then to
Decius the emperor he said, as if inviting him to a meal,
'Thou cursed wretch, thou hast roasted that one side,
turn that other, and eat'.

St Laurence has nearly as many churches in England
as St Margaret.

His feast day is August 10th. Just about that time
every year – August 1st to August 20th – there is a regular
fall of shooting stars. Astronomers call them the Per-
seids, but their popular name was St Laurence's
Tears.

SAINT HELEN. She was the mother of the Emperor Constantine, who asked her to look for the Cross in Jer-

ST CATHERINE AND HER WHEEL

usalem. The secret of its burial place was known to one of the wise men of Jerusalem who refused to reveal it, until he had been seven days in a pit, by Helen's orders, without food or rest. Then he was taken out, and went with St Helen to Golgotha, where 'anon the earth moved, and fume of great sweetness was felt'.

Three crosses were dug up. They decided which of the three was the True Cross by laying a dead body on each in turn. When it was laid on the third cross – the True Cross – the body came to life.

The same wise man – by this time a Christian and Bishop of Jerusalem – was asked by St Helen to look for the nails with which Christ had been nailed to the True Cross. He found them 'shining as gold'. Another story – but this is not included in *The Golden Legend* – claimed that St Helen found in the cave stable in which Christ was born at Bethlehem, the hay which had formed the Virgin Mary's bed and the smock she had worn. These relics she gave to the great church of St Sophia in Constantinople, where they were treasured, until Charlemagne took them to Aix-la-Chapelle (Aachen).

Lady's Bedstraw (Our Lady's Bedstraw), the name for the yellow flower of roadsides in the summer, comes from the hay St Helen was supposed to have found, and the pale Lady's Smock of fields in April and May commemorates in its name the finding of the smock.

St Helen was given more than 100 medieval churches in England.

SAINT NICHOLAS – he must be mentioned, not only as the Christmas saint, Santa Claus, but for the three children in a tub, who identify him. This Bishop of Myra, in Asia Minor, in the time of the Emperor Constantine, was credited with bringing several children back to life, including the three in the tub. It is a pickling tub: at a time of famine in Myra an innkeeper had killed the children, cut them up and salted them down as if they were little pigs.

Sometimes you see this bishop with three golden balls, which were the dowry he gave to save three girls.

St Nicholas has nearly 400 old churches in England.

Some are inland, many are by the sea, because he was also held to have saved the merchants and sailors of a ship from drowning. They invoked St Nicholas, and then saw him floating in the air above the ship just when it was going to founder. 'Anon a man appeared in his likeness, and said: Lo! see ye me not, and then he began to help them in their exploit of the sea, and anon the tempest ceased'.

So St Nicholas became the patron of sailors as well as the patron of children.

There you have four saints who were popular all over Europe. Each country also cherished its own local saints, and as you explore, you will find English saints, Welsh, Cornish and Irish saints; and – not unnaturally, because of William the Conqueror and Hastings, and the French dominions which the English held for so long – saints from France.

A Norman lord of the manor would build a church on his English land. What could he be expected to do but give it into the care of the saint he had been named after as a child in Normandy, who had brought him safe to England and through the battle at Hastings, or some other saint he had been devoted to at home? That must often have happened.

Three French saints you will often come across are ST MARTIN OF TOURS, a favourite in England as well as France, with more than 150 old churches in England (one of them St Martin-in-the-Fields, at the corner of the

National Gallery in London); SAINT GILES, with nearly
as many churches (one of them is St Giles-in-the-Fields,
that London church near Tottenham Court Road,
where 'UNPARALLEL'D PENDEREL' – you will remember I

ST MARTIN OF TOURS

wrote of him at the end of Chapter 3 – is buried in the
grubby churchyard); and ST LEONARD, with more than
150 churches.

ST MARTIN, 'Forefather of the French Nation': he lived
from A.D. 316 to A.D. 397. You cannot miss him in
France or England. He is pictured by the most famous

incident in his life. Riding outside the gates of Amiens one very cold winter day, this young Roman cavalry officer from Hungary met 'a poor man all naked, to whom no man gave any alms'. He 'drew out his sword and carved his mantle herewith in two pieces in the middle, and gave one half to the poor man, for he had nothing else to give him, and he clad himself with that other half'. He dreamt that night that he saw Christ in heaven wearing the half of the cloak which he had given to the beggar, and Christ said to the angels 'Martin, yet new in the faith, hath covered me with this vesture'.

St Martin, who brought the Gauls to Christianity, became Bishop of Tours, in mid-France, which used to be the capital of the early kings of France. At Tours these ancient kings treasured a relic of St Martin, believing that it protected them. It was none other than one of the two halves of Martin's mantle, cloak, or cape – his *cappella*, his 'little cape'. It was looked after by the keepers of the cape, the *cappellani*.

So two common words we use came into existence. The building which housed the *cappella* was itself called The Cappella; which became our two modern words 'chapelle' in French, and 'chapel' in English, for a side-chapel in a church, or a small separate building, where *cappellani*, or *chapelains*, or 'chaplains' officiate.

St Giles, a more shadowy saint, a hermit, from the wilds of the south of France. You see him represented with an arrow sometimes, and almost always with a hind jumping up against him affectionately. He came from Athens, says *The Golden Legend*. He lived in barren desert country which he made fertile. 'And when he had done this miracle he doubted the peril of the glory human, and left that place, and entered farther into the desert and there found a pit' – which means a hollow – 'and a little well, and a fair hind, which without doubt was purveyed of God for to nourish him, and at certain hours ministered her milk to him'.

When the king came with hounds and knights, the hounds did not dare to approach, so one of the knights loosed an arrow at the hind, which missed and wounded old St Giles. He recovered and the king persuaded him to become a bishop.

So you see St Giles with a bishop's crosier as well as a hind and maybe with the arrow which hurt him. St Giles is said to have lived in the sixth or the eighth century.

St Leonard the hermit, who died in 559, was the god-child of Clovis, King of the Franks, and became a good man famous for taking pity on captives and procuring ransom for them. For that reason he holds their chains or fetters in one hand. Like St Giles and St Martin he retreated to the desert, to a hermitage in a deep forest in central France. When he died a miracle related in *The Golden Legend* showed his monks (he had founded a monastery) and his people where he should be buried. They prayed and had nothing to eat for three days. 'And on the third day they saw all the country covered with snow, save only the place wherein St Leonard would rest, which was all void'.

Norman lords owned the great forest of St Leonard in Sussex. Hermits lived in this forest, and Sussex people believed that one of them had been St Leonard himself. He killed a dragon there, and Lilies of the Valley, known in Sussex as Leonard's Lilies, are supposed to have grown up where drops of the dragon's blood fell to the ground.

Another saint to remember is St Michael, that arch-angel and captain of the host of heaven. You will find that many of his six hundred and more churches and chapels are on hill tops. Like St Michael's Mount in Cornwall, or Mont-St-Michel across the Channel, in Brittany.

Why? Partly because in the Middle Ages men

MONT-ST-MICHEL, BRITTANY

believed that St Michael several times flew down from heaven, alighting on high ground and hills; partly because British Christians in Wales and Cornwall had learnt a special veneration for St Michael from the desert monks in Egypt. In Egypt they had transferred to St Michael some of the attributes of Osiris, the old Egyptian god. Osiris had weighed the souls of men after their death. St Michael was supposed to do the same. Osiris was the god of the light of the sun. Egyptian monks thought of St Michael as the archangel of the sun, and often they would cap their monasteries with a chapel dedicated to St Michael, placed so that it would sparkle in the first rays of the morning sun.

A chapel or a church on a hill, on Mont-St-Michel or St Michael's Mount or Glastonbury Tor (where only the tower remains of St Michael's church) would catch the light of heaven in the same way, morning and evening.

And do not forget the specially British and Irish and specially English saints. There were holy men who went backwards and forwards between Wales, Cornwall and Brittany, some thirteen hundred to fifteen hundred years ago, leaving their names behind in churches and parishes. In Cornwall a village or parish name will often begin with Lan–, in Wales with Llan–, followed by a saint's name. A *llan* was an enclosure. Each of these *lans* or *llans* will have been, first of all, a little enclosure for monks or hermit-monks consecrated actually by the saint whose name it bears.

If you come to a Llandewi in Wales it will have been founded by that Welsh saint we all know about, Dewi Sant, St David, who lived in the sixth century. You will know that Dewi Sant was actually there, in the sun or the rain.

These saints, too, have their lives and legends, their wonder stories of crossing the sea on a leaf or a stone, of taming fierce wolves or making holy springs break from the ground, or healing lepers or bringing the dead to life.

Ireland and Scotland have their saints, Patrick and Bridget and Colum Cille (whom the Scottish call St Columba), Brandan, Ninian, Kentigern. England has her very English saints – to be encountered especially in the Midlands, in East Anglia, and in the North-East – whom most English people seem to know nothing about any more, though of course, we don't forget the more famous of them such as the Venerable Bede (whom our ancestors used to call St Bede), or St Cuthbert, or St Swithun.

The Norman Conquest is really to blame. There were only a few centuries in which the fame of the English saints could grow. Then the Normans arrived, and with them more and more of those now familiar saints of France, who became so important to Medieval Englishmen.

Let's take two who are well-known, and one who isn't, to give a taste of what you may find about English saints, and about wonder tales here at home.

ST CUTHBERT, the holy man of Durham Cathedral, which became his shrine, and was dedicated to St Mary and St Cuthbert. He is the saint of many more north-eastern churches. Think of Cuthbert as a hermit on the Farne Islands (where he died in 687), praying with 'St Cuthbert's Chickens', the black and white eiderduck, comfortable alongside him in their nests of eiderdown – birds he would allow no one to hurt or kill.

Or think of the wonder tale of Cuthbert and the two otters. Cuthbert, when he was at Coldingham in Berwickshire, spent the night praying in the sea, the waves coming up to his shoulders and his neck. He walked ashore at dawn, and knelt on the sand and two otters came up and licked his feet, and then dried them and warmed them with their fur.

One account says that when he came to the beach 'he could not stand for feebleness and faintness', and fell on the ground, whereon the otters 'came and licked every place of his body'.

ST GUTHLAC, the hermit of the Isle of Crowland, in the Fens, in 'the drownèd lands of Lincolnshire'. Crowland Abbey was dedicated to Saint Mary, St Bartholomew and St Guthlac, who had once robbed and killed as one of the wild soldiers of Ethelred, king of Mercia. Then he became a monk, and after a while retreated to the Fens, at Crowland (he died there in 714), among the reeds and the black water and winds. There he prayed and resisted demons, fed birds, beasts, and fishes, and talked to two swallows which sat and sang on his shoulder.

ST WYSTAN. Have you ever met anybody called Wystan after this unfamiliar saint from Shropshire or Leicestershire? The most famous living English poet is W. H. Auden, Wystan Hugh Auden, whose uncle was rector of Wistanstow, where St Wystan was killed in 849. There is little to know of Wystan, but that little is rather wonderful. He was a child who had succeeded to the kingdom of Mercia, though he wanted to be a monk instead of a king. Either at Wistow, in Leicestershire, or at Wistanstow, in Shropshire (both these names mean Wystan's Church), he arranged to meet and make peace with his uncle who wanted to be king; and his uncle's son, as he gave Wystan the kiss of peace, cut open his head with a sword and killed him.

For thirty days a column of light rose into the sky from the field where he was murdered, and every year on the anniversary of the murder the severed hairs of Wystan's head grew up again out of the ground.

Saints, you see, are not just a matter of hymns, collects, Sundays, and Scripture.

To find out about the saint or saints of your parish church or your neighbourhood, the first book to consult is a dictionary of saints. Try the 'Penguin Dictionary of Saints'** by Donald Attwater (1965). And try – it is very entertaining, but much shorter – 'A Travellers Guide to Saints in Europe'*, by Mary Sharp (1964).

The trouble is that writers about saints – and especially people who put them into dictionaries – are sometimes scornful about the wonder side of the legends of the saints, however famous, who may not really have existed. I think this is a pity, since tall stories can be good to read, and anyhow it is interesting to know about the kind of story our ancestors enjoyed. Perhaps the otters never wiped and warmed St Cuthbert's feet on the beach, but I don't think that knowing the story about them harms you, me, or St Cuthbert.

You may be lucky and find that you can see or borrow or even buy a modern edition of Caxton's translation of that 'Golden Legend' I have mentioned so often. A charming edition in seven little volumes, edited by F. S. Ellis, who knew all about the poetry of the lives of the saints, was published in the Temple Classics in 1900. That may be in your public library. It is the best and the most delightful way of finding out about famous saints such as St Catherine or St Margaret or St George or St Nicholas.

Caxton's translation was published in 1483, so it was among the first 20 or so books in our language ever to be printed.

Caxton did add a few English saints; lives, for instance, of St Cuthbert, and St Swithun the rain saint of Winchester, St Alphege who came from Gloucestershire, St Kenelm who was murdered at Clent in Staffordshire —

In Clent in Cowbage, Kenelm, king born
Lieth under a thorn,
His head off shorn —

And East Anglia's St Edmund, King and Martyr, whose head was cut off his dead body by the Danes, was diligently guarded by a great wolf, 'sitting and embracing the head between his forelegs, keeping it from all other

*beasts' (you can often see St Edmund and the Wolf in
East Anglian churches.)*

*But Caxton and 'The Golden Legend' are only a lim-
ited help. To find out much about English – and Welsh
and Irish and Cornish saints, and Scottish saints, and
many of the less than famous saints – you will need to be
even more of a ferret in your public library, trying
among other things dictionaries and encyclopaedias
about Christianity, the great 'Dictionary of National
Biography' and the 'Dictionary of Welsh National Biography'.*

*Guidebooks may help, and of course you will discover
clues to books and lives in that 'Penguin Dictionary of
Saints'. Another useful book is 'Anglo-Saxon Saints and
Scholars', by E. S. Duckett (1947).*

*Then more strictly about saints and the churches dedi-
cated to them, the public library will probably have
'Dedications and Patron Saints of English Churches', by
Francis Bond (1914); and it might have the rather uncommon three volumes of 'Studies in Church Dedications or England's Patron Saints', by Francis Arnold-
Foster (1899). I hope so, because these volumes are a
wonder-chest of facts about every saint ever commemorated in England.*

*By the way I have not said anything in this chapter
about the way saints are or have been 'canonized', that is
to say declared by church authority to have been saints.
You can discover about canonization and when it began
in an official way, and exactly what it means, in the first
pages of that 'Penguin Dictionary of Saints'.*

6

THE TALE OF A COTTAGE

HAVE you ever looked round your house, noticing plates and cups and jugs and vases, saucepans and fire-irons and vacuum cleaner, things made of earthenware and glass and metal and plastic, and then wondered what has become of everything used about the houses of the village or the town in all the past centuries?

Perhaps the place where you live has an Old English name, showing it existed long before William conquered the English in 1066. Perhaps it was inhabited before the English arrived; perhaps before the coming of the Romans, when the British had no one to interfere with them.

Where has everything gone, from their buildings to their spoons?

You must reckon that most buildings, most houses, around you will not be very ancient. Villages of stone are not as old as they look. For one thing, the more ancient houses were not built very durably. Stone was quarried for churches and abbeys and castles and important houses. Ordinary people – in the countryside or the small towns – did not make much use of stone for their houses until the sixteenth century or the seventeenth. Instead they built themselves little cots of wattle-and-daub; which was a frame woven of willow or of hazel, daubed and slapped and smoothed with a mixture of clay and horse-dung and perhaps a little lime. The cots were so frail and thin that a man sitting indoors could be murdered by a spear thrust in through the wall.

In other places they might build up their homes with layer on top of layer of cob, which is a primitive concrete – clay mixed with chopped straw, small stones, and cow hair.

These houses of wattle-and-daub or of cob were roofed with a straw thatch, which is the oldest of coverings. Indeed, at one time whole towns were thatched. Even now in a few older towns (Shaftesbury on top of a hill in Dorset is one of them) a few thatched roofs still exist between roofs of tile and slate, suggesting that towns must once have looked like kraals in Africa.

Thatch decays, rain and frost attack timbering and cob and wattle-and-daub, and the primitive cot falls down, or is pulled down; and a new cot goes up – and so on, until at last, in a later century, the time comes to build more strongly in stone.

In Chapter 3 I mentioned the initials and the date R. S. 1625 in my own house. I suspect that R.S. in 1625 put up a house of stone in place of an old house in wattle-and-daub. He still used wattle-and-daub to divide some of the rooms; which is awkward, since it is not very firm, when we want to hang things on the wall. Underneath the stone floors which R.S. put in, I suppose there might be traces of the older house.

It is rather the same with churches. What is under the floor? Dead men's bones, of course; in coffins here and there, or in a vault (do you know *Moonfleet*, by Meade Falkner, and the chapter about the doings in the vault of Moonfleet church, and how John Trenchard found himself clutching the black wiry beard of one of the dead Mohuns?). But under one church there may also be remains of another church, and another, and another. Under St Bride's church, off Fleet Street in London, or

rather under the latest St Bride's church, which Sir
Christopher Wren built in 1680, and then under the
remains of the medieval St Bride's church, traces have
actually been found of the original little British church
which was first dedicated there to St Bride, who is the
holy Bridget of Ireland.

Still, you cannot go digging for the past under your

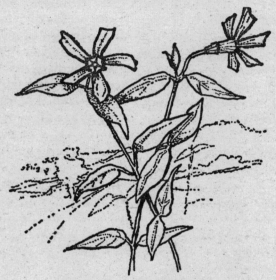

LESSER PERIWINKLE

parish church, or under your own kitchen floor. But
places do exist where you can dig probably without hin-
drance (and without upsetting archaeologists, who do
not like amateurs to destroy evidence in important
places), and where things are to be found. Things not
very old, but oldish; evidences at any rate, of a way of
living that does not exist any more, counting 'old' just as
a century or two.

Look for the sites of cottages away from the village

which stood by themselves somewhere on the edges of the parish.

Here the maps of Chapter 1 are going to be useful. A small cottage such as I mentioned in that chapter may have been abandoned at any time in the last hundred or hundred and fifty years. Probably it will be shown by one of the maps – though not the newer ones. Or there will be clues remaining on the ground. There may still be a scrap of a lane going to the site. The collapse of the cottage may have left a mound. There may be a yew tree still flourishing where it was planted (generally to the south-west) to shelter and protect the house. Or a few old orchard trees – plum, bullace, apple – may survive; or a few gooseberry bushes, or a clump of box, or hardy plants from the garden which persist in spite of brambles and nettles – snowdrops early in the year, or poisonous blue monkshood, or soapwort, or an old rose, or periwinkle.

Edward Thomas, a poet who liked every intriguing overgrown corner in a field, wrote a poem about such a cottage, or cottage site, which he called *A Tale*:

There once the walls
Of the ruined cottage stood.
The periwinkle crawls
With flowers in its hair into the wood.

In flowerless hours
Never will the bank fail
With everlasting flowers
On fragments of blue plates, to tell the tale.

The fragments of blue plates are part of what you have come for (which reminds me to remind you always to bring something to grub with, a small garden fork, a trowel, especially a small mason's trowel, or a small iron bar – something fairly light which will fit into a haversack).

As well as scraps of plate and bowl and cup with coloured designs which were applied from transfers, you are sure to come upon remains of old glass bottles, scraps of Staffordshire teapot, pieces of hard stoneware, and slipware prettily decorated with patterns like curly printer's brackets, in dark brown on yellow. Also bulky fragments of earthenware crock, red and rough on one side, glazed green or greenish-yellow on the side which was the inside.

And there will be bowls and stems of clay pipes. Possibly some of the pipe bowls will be stamped on the pro-

CLAY PIPES AND STAMPS

jecting piece at the bottom with the maker's initials and the date.

Sometimes enough will be traceable of the walls or the foundations of the cottage to tell where the front door was – or back door, if it had one.

Now imagine. You have broken a crock, or a plate. Instead of being tidy (why bother about tidiness – you ought to, but that is another matter – out in this lonely cottage, without neighbours?), you go to the door and you fling the bits away, with your right hand.

That is where the bits will be, about flinging distance

away, to the right of the door. That is the place to grub
or excavate.

I have picked up or excavated or grubbed up a
number of things which told me about life in such cottages – not only scraps of china and glazed earthenware,
but spindle-whorls made of stone (the women were
always spinning, to add to the man's miserable wages); a
reaping hook or sickle of the kind used in the harvest, the
kind which is half of the national emblem – the hammer
and sickle – of the Russians; an iron crock or cauldron
with legs, such as was slung over the fire in the open
hearth; and a tiny pair of bronze nutcrackers, with
which dead and gone cottagers cracked hazel-nuts and
filberts. And standing on my table, while I write this
chapter and watch out for commas and misspellings, I
have a little figure of white china, gilded and coloured.
He comes from the rubbish heap of an old cottage,
chucked away because someone had knocked his head
off.

He wears gaiters, orange shoes, and orange knee-
breeches and a short smock – like one of the cottagers.
One day I hope to spot his counterpart, head and all, in
a museum, and so learn for sure when (I expect it was
about 1800), and exactly where, he was made.

Yet in a public museum, or in the folk museum among
the bygones illustrating cottage life, whole and un-
broken in glass cases where they cannot be picked up
and examined, all such objects are far less exciting. Far
better the broken bits and pieces, which *you* have found
in *your own* museum, in *your own* room (your own
museum is something to think about in the last chapter).

Also, once more, don't be a snob about oldness. These
cottage bits and pieces will be true archaeological finds
as much as a gold cup out of the tomb of a queen at Ur

of the Chaldees. From the site of the cottage hidden away across the fields, they have plenty to say of hard lives before bicycles and cars and buses and bakers, of days when people went to bed with the sun, or at the most lit the cottage in the winter with rushlights made from the pith of rushes dipped in tallow, and held in an iron clip.

And if we are going to be archaeological, the tale of the lonely abandoned cottage with a spring flowing alongside for water supply will have begun centuries before those scraps of blue china.

Edward Thomas in his poem talks of the periwinkle

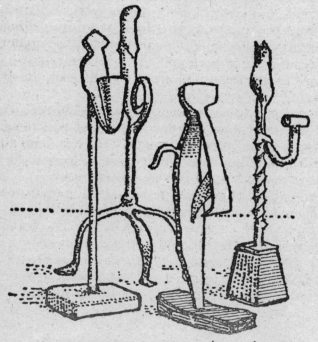

RUSHLIGHT HOLDERS (RIGHT)
AND (CANDLEHOLDERS) (LEFT)

at his cottage site crawling into the wood. Now that is just right. Perhaps the cottage which the china and earthenware comes from was built about 1670, perhaps it was abandoned in 1850, or in 1900. But there may have been cottages there before. The site may have been an 'assart', a piece of waste land or of woodland right out on the edge of the manor which a hard-working peasant with hands as tough as an oak log cleared by permission of the lord of the manor as long ago, say, as 1200 or 1300. And there he may have built himself one of those clay or wattle-and-daub cots with a thatched roof and a mud floor and a hole in the thatch to carry off the smoke.

From the map you may be able to work out how large a piece of land was taken in from the wood, which may have vanished altogether or may still be there alongside. Old maps, old documents, may tell you the name of the cottage, the name by which the assart was originally known ('assart' itself is from an Old French word *es-sarter*, meaning to grub up).

Of course, it is not so likely that you will come across anything which belonged to the families who lived on the assart in the Middle Ages. It would be deep down under the debris of the later cottage. Remember, also, that the ancient cottagers would not have been at all well off in their dark smoky hovel with its mud floor and its little wooden-shuttered opening for windows.

They would not have used much earthenware or so many things made of metal. Their own platters and bowls they would have carved from wood (especially from beech wood). Just as the Greeks and Romans used skins for wine, so they made jugs out of ox-hide. And for mugs and beakers they had horn from their cows and oxen.

Wood, horn, leather, all decay and disappear.

With luck some of the bits of white or coloured crockery from an old cottage will have the maker's name or initials or his mark on the underside. Draw the mark, or if it has been pressed into the surface, make a rubbing of it with a soft pencil over a thin piece of paper. Then off to the library and search for the mark or name in the 'Handbook of Pottery and Porcelain Marks' by J. B. Cushion and W. B. Honey (1956).

You are pretty certain to come across pieces of Willow Pattern, which are still being made, and was first made about 1775–1780.

It will not be quite so easy to find out about clay pipes, The pipe-maker may have stamped his initials, his whole name, and even the date on the heel underneath the bowl of the pipe.

Your museum should have details of local pipe-makers. And there, or at the library, you may be able to look at Volume xxiii of the 'Journal of the British Archaeological Association (1960), in which there are lists by Adrian Oswald of English pipe-makers, which should tell you who was making clay pipes in your neighbourhood in the eighteenth century and in the seventeenth century when everyone began to smoke. (By the way if you name is Piper or if you have a friend called Piper, it won't be because his ancestor or yours made clay pipes, but because he played on the bagpipes, which used to be common everywhere, not only in Scotland and Ireland.)

Of course pipes and recognizable scraps of pottery do not turn up only on the site of an old cottage. Keep an eye open in your own garden. Always look along a newly cleared ditch in the fields and along newly ploughed or harrowed fields. Often, too, men will be digging out foundations for a house or a garage, or cutting into a bank, or widening a road.

This chapter mentions rushlights and Edward Thomas. Museums often have iron rushlight holders from a cottage. In the 'Natural History of Selborne' (which I spoke about in Chapter 2) Gilbert White says enough about rushlights to enable you to make your own – though you will need to be able to recognize the right kind of rush, the Soft Rush, or Juncus *effusus. A rushlight 2 feet 4 inches long, Gilbert White says, will burn nearly an hour.*

Edward Thomas's 'Collected Poems'* you may enjoy. His friend Walter de la Mare said that he liked everything from heaths and roads and woods to flints and dust. So his poems are about everything – owls and plovers, and mangolds, morning and evening, snow, paths, rain, ponds, moorhens, mill-wheels, streams, chalk-pits, even dust on nettles.

7

ANATHOTHS AND MANORS
AND MILLS

MAPS again. On your largest scale map you can fill in all your discoveries, indeed everything you cannot actually collect, and a good deal that you can.

For instance, the whereabouts of an uncommon flower, say wild daffodil or wild columbine, can be marked. Or you can mark the whereabouts of the best echoes. On echoes, by the way, Gilbert White again wrote several pages in his book about Selborne. He used to go and speak Latin verses to the echo and he has a strange word for 'a place of responses or echoes' – anathoth, which looks Egyptian, but is Greek, and only means, after all, a 'coming back'.

Anyhow, mark your anathoths, and read what Gilbert White says about them.

Since we were talking in the last chapter about an assart out on the edge of the manor, I suggest discovering as well all that there is to be discovered about the manor in your village, your parish, your neighbourhood, even your part of the town, which may have grown street by street over the fields of a manor.

Plenty of books say what a manor was. Really it was a way of organizing life and crops and land, going back at any rate to Norman days. I think you could almost say that a manor was a stage backwards towards living in a tribe, with tribal chief; though a lord of the manor was, at his most powerful, rather a brute; he was a dictator on a small scale whom the peasants on the manor had to obey in many things; and they could not get rid of him at will.

A medieval lord of the manor may lie cold and stony in the church, with his nose knocked off, poor effigy of a man, and with names and dates scribbled over his face and his armour.

If your village still centres around a manor-house, around the home of the former lord surviving now like a fossil out of times forgotten and gone, then other surviving or enduring fossils of the manor are likely to be at hand.

Do you know of fields divided into wide parallel ridges (easier to recognize in the evening, when every slight rise casts a shadow)?

Do you know where to find the pound, the mill, the dovecote?

If so, you are on the track.

The assart will have been grubbed up, remember, on the outskirts of the manor, from the waste or the woods where the lord's men could run their cows and their pigs and where they were entitled to as much wood as they could gather (origin of a phrase we use every day) 'by hook or by crook', without using an axe. Close in to the manor-house and the village there will have been great open fields; originally (and here and there still) without hedges.

The lord's men, the ancestors of the village people of today, had their selions, their strips, in these fields. As they ploughed these fairly narrow strips, the plough threw the earth inward a little. So as the centuries went by, the strips tended to rise in the middle almost into ridges.

In many counties these old ploughlands, now under

grass, are very easy to spot. And it is no trouble to mark them on the map. People will tell you, of course, that the fields were divided like that so as to drain them. If the field is flat, water does gather between strip and strip and encourage rushes to grow.

But see how often the strips cross sloping ground, which could be ploughed, of course, but certainly never had to be drained.

In such fields (often divided from the huge open fields into smaller modern fields with hedges of elm or hazel) you are looking upon all that is left of the old face of England, moulded and shaped by the tread of peasants and their slow oxen pulling a rough wooden plough.

Lords of the manor liked to organize everything for their own benefit. Each manor had a pound – something which survives in the word 'impound', which is not infrequently heard from schoolmasters ('I shall impound that object').

Into the pound went the stray animals on the manor, which could do much damage on the great open hedgeless fields; and to retrieve your animals you paid a fine –

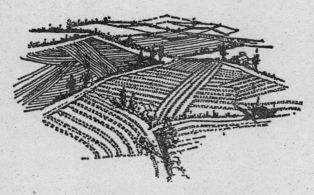

PLOUGHLAND AND STRIPS

to the lord. Pounds were roughly rectangular enclosures with a high wall. You can make them out sometimes by a stream or spring, convenient for watering the impounded cattle, which would tread quite a depth of lane between the pound and the water.

On that stream the lord of the manor owned his corn mill. Or in streamless country he would own a later invention, a windmill. If as a tenant of the manor you had corn to grind, then it was a rule that it must be ground for you at the lord's mill – or he knew the reason why, and fined you again.

Also the lord, and the lord alone, had a pigeon-house or dove-house or dovecote: his pigeons might eat your peas or beans or young corn, but there was trouble if they were killed – if, in short, you interfered with the prospects of his pigeon pie or his squab pie of young pigeons from the square nesting holes in the pigeon-house.

If he lived by the sea, instead of spending money on a sturdy, round dovecote the lord would sometimes wall in a sea-cave or a narrow slit in the cliffs and fit it up with stone nesting-boxes. There is a strange Culver Hole like that ('culver' being the old name for pigeon) in the cliffs of Gower peninsular in South Wales.

Ploughlands, mills, dovecotes – whereabouts as well did they hold the fair, the rights of which would also have belonged to his lordship? And is there by any chance a stone lock-up, a blind-house, standing all by itself, with a door and no windows, somewhere near the fair ground, handy for anyone drunk who 'broke the peace of the fair'?

Of all the relics of the manor, the mills are my own favourite, especially the water-mills, the oldest form of machine for power in England, where we have had them since Anglo-Saxon times.

Even when the mill has vanished, there are usually
traces to be seen – perhaps the old millpond, now dry or
merely damp, perhaps the pit in which the wheel re-
volved, perhaps the leat cut from the stream along the
side of the valley to bring the water to the top of the
wheel; perhaps a few old millstones.

Or the wheel may have been undershot, not overshot.
That is to say, instead of working by the weight of water
falling over the top into its buckets, the wheel will have

A POST MILL

been pushed round by the current flowing underneath.
This is the kind of mill for slower streams with a good
volume of water. Often (in rather a dull way) the wheel
will be inside the mill-house. Or such an undershot
wheel may be pushed round by water imprisoned – or
impounded – from the high tide in an estuary. (Also,

though it did not belong in the same way to the manor, you may have had a tucking-mill or a fulling-mill in your parish – a waterwheel which raised wooden

A TOWER MILL

'perches' like heavy flails, to beat, or tuck, or full the new-made cloth, i.e. make it full by compacting the fibres. Hence the names Tucker or Fuller for the men who worked mills of the kind.)

The Greeks invented the water-mill about two thousand years ago. Arabs (or so it appears) invented the windmill about a thousand or eleven hundred years later. Your windmill may have been a post mill, with its buck, or body, and machinery and sails all mounted, so that they could be turned into the wind, on a great wooden post. Or it may have been a slender tower mill, or a timber-framed smock mill, of which only the top, with the sails, needed to be turned.

Even if nothing is left of your windmill, you may still discover the green mound built up as a foundation for it on top of some Windmill Hill. Sometimes, instead of building a mound, the millwrights used a prehistoric round barrow.

Other things? How about searching for such items around you (if you have them) as fords and pack-bridges (narrow, for taking a string of pack-horses when too much water flows over the ford) and toll-houses and upping-stocks (from which the extra passenger upped into her pillion behind the rider on horseback)? How about locating the tithe-barn, in which the parson stored his tithe or tenth of the crops which the farmers had to give him; or the old skittle alley?

How about searching for all the wells and springs (including perhaps holy wells, also springs impregnated with minerals, and springs which will turn sticks and oddments to stone, by coating them with calcium carbonate)?

Or plotting the old withy-beds, which were planted and kept and cut by basket-makers; or the old fish-weirs on the river?

Why not explore canals and their locks and supply ponds (lock-gates were invented by Leonardo da Vinci)? Or dewponds on the downs? Or the follies – sham ruins – and prospect towers and grottoes built, probably between 1750 and 1850, by rich landlords?

Or old limekilns, which were often placed on beaches or up a tidal river, so that barges could bring the lime-stone, and the coal for burning it to lime? Here there is a special link between limekilns and your Ordnance Survey maps. Making the maps was pushed forward because of the threat of invasion by the French in Napoleon's time. Many of the limekilns were built at the time of the French wars because we needed more food, which meant the farmer ploughing more land and requiring more lime to sweeten it for his crops.

What about exploring all the footpaths which next to no one uses, now that there are bicycles, motor bicycles, cars, and buses?

Or have you ever walked (it may be a bit of a job if you live in a hilly country) *all around* the boundaries of your parish? That used to be done (more or less, at any rate), when the bounds were beaten on Rogation Days, before Ascension Day. There were processions, the Cross was carried round, village people wore garlands of flowers, the crops were blest, and the priest and the people would stop under a Holy Oak (do you remember about St Boniface and the Oak?) or Gospel Oak on the parish boundary, and the gospel would be read, and bells would be rung to frighten away demons; and the bounds would be beaten with sticks (also to scare the demons).

And sometimes, at a difficult point a boy would be beaten as well as the bounds, to make him remember all his life exactly where the parish boundary ran.

The most enjoyable book I know about manors is 'Life on the English Manor 1150–1400',* by H. S. Bennett (1937), which starts off with an imaginary week in the hard life of a peasant in his manor village.

W. G. Hoskins knows everything about the surface of

England, and there are a thousand facts in a book by
him, 'The Making of the English Landscape'* (1955).

Some books about other things in this chapter are:
Gilbert Sheldon, 'From Track to Turnpike' (1928); A. J.
Pugsley, 'Dewponds in Fable and Fact' (1939);* Barbara Jones, 'Follies and Grottoes' (1953).

All you need to know about windmills Rex Wailes
(who is an engineer from a family of millwrights) has
put into 'The English Windmill'* (1954). I am afraid
there is no good book about water-mills – yet.

For canals look at 'British Canals', by Charles
Hadfield* (1950). And you should be able to learn fascinating things about your local canal, if it has not been
too long abandoned, from an old copy of 'Bradshaw's
Canals and Navigable Rivers of England and Wales'. It
gives facts as well about the kinds of barge, about locks,
lifts, tunnels, aqueducts; and it includes a canal glossary
– my 1928 copy does, at any rate – explaining such
words as 'chalico', 'gongoozler', 'stanks', 'staunches',
'cloughs', 'slackers', 'loodel'; and 'legging', which is
pushing a barge through a tunnel with your legs –
against the roof.

I meant to have a chapter about names of places, but
there is going to be no room for more than a note, for
which the end of this chapter is the right place.

First of all, it is pleasant to know the meaning of the
name of the place you live in (not always though; for
instance, if you live in Swindon, it is perhaps pleasanter
not to know that it means Pig Hill).

Since words change and names get transformed after
centuries, you cannot often take place-names to mean
what they seem to mean. Scholars expert in Old Celtic,
Old English and Old Norse look for the meaning in the
much earlier, purer, and simpler forms of a place-name
which may survive in ancient documents.

The names of English towns and counties and parishes and rivers (and much else) are explained by Dr Ekwall in his 'Concise Oxford Dictionary of English Placenames'.*

Explorations of the kind I have been suggesting in this chapter will be easier if you know the names of all the fields, corners, roads, lanes, streets, ponds, streams, springs, and so on round your home. Such names will give clue after clue.

For instance, a chapel of the Middle Ages may have been pulled down centuries ago. But the farmer may still call the field Chapel Close or Chapel Field, and if you know which field it is, you may be able to see from humps in the grass exactly where the chapel stood; or you may be able to find pieces of cut stone from the chapel built into a hedge or a wall.

When the Tithe Maps were made for each parish, the farms were listed field by field, name by name, with numbers referring to the map. The vicar or rector may still have that Tithe Apportionment, as well as the map. If so, you can write in all the field names on your own map.

For many counties there is a volume (made for the English Place-Name Society) explaining names, parish by parish. Suppose you live in a town, in your county volume you will find the name of the town explained, then the older street names. If you live in a country parish, there will be your parish name, and the names of the farms, which may be a thousand years old or more; and a good many of the names of the fields as well.

I like to come upon names telling of animals or birds we no longer have — beavers or wolves or the kite. Names, too, about old gods, Tiw, Woden, Thunor, and Frig (the gods of Tuesday, Wednesday, Thursday, and Friday); and about goblins and demons, hobs and thyrsts and pucks, who have given names to fields and paths and ponds and nooks and caves — Hobhole, for example, or Puckstye, which means Puck's Path, or Thursford, which means ford where a thyrst or goblin lived.

Mind, there was nothing small or airy-fairy about such creatures. They were man-sized, so it was thought, and terrible to meet. Remember Grendel, killed by Beowulf; he was one of them, living deep below a mere or a black pool. In Wiltshire there still exists a small pond which the Anglo-Saxons called Grendel's Mere.

8

FLINTS AND SHERDS AND
PRESERVATIONS BELOW THE MOON

TWENTY thousand years ago mammoths with hides three-quarters of an inch thick, hung with long bristly reddish hair, and fat rhinoceroses covered with wool, fed across as much of England as was not covered with ice – a cold, damp, stormy England with few trees, but much grass and many flowers (including marsh marigolds) in the short summer.

If they wished to stroll from England to Holland, there was nothing to stop them – since there was no channel and not a great deal of North Sea – unless on the way they were trapped in pits by some of the very few hunting tribes, who also wandered about the ice-free parts of England (and Wales), sheltering and sometimes burying their dead in caves in the limestone.

The weather grew warmer, the dirty edges of the great glaciers crumbled and melted, new land appeared from under the ice and forests began to grow and spread, and the animals which were used neither to warmth nor to forest, kept as near as they could, to the shrinking glaciers. They withdrew eastwards towards Denmark, over land which was first freed of ice, then swallowed by the rising seas.

Under the North Sea is the Dogger Bank. When fishermen began to trawl over the Bank, their trawls moving to and fro across the bottom were fouled and damaged by peaty chunks of the old land surface, which the fishermen called 'moorlog'. Bones came up in the trawl, of mammoth and woolly rhinoceros and reindeer and wild horse and bison and wild oxen. The Dogger Bank had been the upper limit of the drowned lands of the North Sea, and had disappeared inch by inch under salt water about nine thousand years ago, or 7000 B.C.

Earlier ice-meltings had scoured away some of the ridge of chalk between England and France. But the freeze-up had returned, bringing the mammoths and the hunters. The sea-level had dropped again, and what was left of the ridge still made a dry passage to France. When the glaciers melted again at the end of the Old Stone Age, the rising waters not only swamped the North Sea lands but forced a newer, deeper passage through the pale chalk between Beachy Head and Cap Gris Nez; and the island we have was created.

Exactly when?

Well, nearer 6000 B.C. than 7000 B.C. We have now been an island for about eight thousand years; and below the channel boat which takes us to Calais there lies the bare, scoured, chalky base of that old ridge or bridge.

Many more than twenty thousand years ago flint tools and weapons were being made in that England of the Old Stone Age, which endured until the glaciers melted. In a Middle Stone Age from about 10,000 B.C. fishermen and huntsmen around the marshes – few enough of them, though now a larger population – still used flint.

After the English Channel was cut (a long while after) farmers of the New Stone Age crossed a channel which was still much narrower than the one we have to face, bringing with them in their boats their heifers and bulls and pigs and sheep (all of them rather small breeds) and

their goats and their dogs, and sacks – or pots – of grain
for sowing.

This was some five thousand years ago – about 3000
B.C.

These rough farmers still made tools of flint and
other hard kinds of stone. In spite of a knowledge of
metal, so did the Bronze Age people whose age in Britain
begins about 1800 or 1900 B.C.

Now, after all that, can you – you yourself – find flint
tools and weapons about on the surface of England,
Wales, Scotland?

You can, as I said chapters ago – if you look for them;
and really look, with patience; and, of course, if you look
in the right kind of place. One broad rule is that there
are more flint tools to be found on upland country than
in the low valleys and low plains which were anciently
covered with forests of oak.

I found my first flints altogether by accident, at a time
when I never dreamt that I should ever be able to find
such things at all; and never dreamt that they could
exist only four hundred yards away from my home. One
day in the Easter holidays I had visited a lonely barn out
in the fields, hoping that a barn-owl might have laid her
eggs up in the loft (she had).

Then it rained; and after the rain I leant over a gate
looking, in the sunshine, at a field full of barrows. The
field had just been ploughed; and off a something out in
the brown earth the sunlight was sparkling and exploding.

It was a flint – not just a piece of flint but a scraper
shaped like a half-moon, with an edge very finely
chipped and quite regular. My thumb fitted, as I held
this scraper between finger and thumb, comfortably into
a hollow.

Quickly I discovered there were pieces of flint all over

the field, round the burial mounds and on top of them; and later, after a morning's hard search, I found – not at all by accident this time – my first flint arrowhead, with barbs (though most of one barb had broken off).

I must say three things about that good luck and its consequences.

First of all I found those flints in Cornwall. In Cornwall there is no chalk, so there are not flints by nature all over Cornish fields as there are, say in Kent or Wiltshire or Berkshire or much of East Anglia. In a flint country chipped or worked flints are more difficult to spot.

Next, I found the flints near the burial mounds. I searched around other burial mounds and soon collected more flints – and concluded – quite reasonably – that worked flints were always likely to occur somewhere near barrows, because the dead would be buried somewhere near places frequented by the living (just as our own churchyards and churches and homes go together, more or less).

Perhaps it would always be sensible to search the ground – try it anyhow – *east* of barrows, because archaeologists have suggested that barrows may have been placed to the *west* of habitations, since the west is the direction of the setting sun and the Country of the Dead.

Thirdly, these first flints of mine belonged to the Bronze Age, and they were near, and among, and on top of Bronze Age round barrows which had been piled over the burnt remains of the dead. One thing is clear from the huge number of these round barrows – that by 1000 B.C. the population was no longer so very small. In the cold grimness of the time of the glacier and the mammoths, at the end of the Old Stone Age, there were seldom more than seven or eight hundred people altogether in all of England and Wales. In the Bronze Age and just before in the New Stone Age, these few hundreds had gone up to thousands.

So if you search for worked flints, the ones you come across are most likely to be the ones which were made and dropped by New Stone Age men and Bronze Age men.

How about recognizing your flints?

By the time of the New Stone Age and the Bronze Age, the flints were contrived more skilfully and carefully for many purposes – adzing and chopping (especially chopping down trees to clear a piece of ground here and there for corn), cutting, planing, scraping, boring, shaving, rasping – and killing. A Bronze Age arrowhead is neat and recognizable at once. So are such things, not so often picked up, as flint daggers and sickles and axes.

FLINT ARROWHEADS OF THE BRONZE AGE

Small tools fashioned of flakes and then trimmed along the edge – these will give you trouble, at first, unless you are very different from other people, you will start picking up scraps of stone which are not flint, but which look vaguely as if a man had shaped them; and you will be picking up flints on which all the flaking and chipping has occurred naturally.

Books about stone tools are often as dry and stony as the tools themselves, and difficult to follow. Illustrations help. But the thing is to have, in your hands, early on, a few humanly shaped pieces, New Stone Age or Bronze Age. After that, after seeing, for example, what an edge looks like and feels like when it has been carefully and quite regularly trimmed, you will soon be certain of the difference between accident and manufacture.

Don't despise flints. Fashioning flint tools and weapons was not so easy. For one thing the knappers (to *knap*, a quick word for a quick action, is to knock and chip: knappers are flint choppers) were not content with any lump of flint that happened to be lying about.

When they could obtain it, they liked the best and purest material which would flake obediently in the right way and which would not crack or break too easily when it came to using the finished tool.

So flint was mined in the New Stone Age and into the Bronze Age; and at Grimes Graves, not far from Thetford, in Norfolk, you can disappear down a shaft, down a ladder, forty feet underground, into the darkness and mystery of ancient flint mines in the chalk. You can crawl with a candle into the white galleries the miners cut along the veins of flint (and come out with candle grease all over you, and with white knees and elbows and back). You can see how the miners edged and eased out lumps of the best flint as black as coal and a thousand times as hard, using picks contrived from the antlers of red deer.

These were some of the first mines of the world.

With flints there are also sherds of ancient pottery for the finding. When he bakes clay into pots, the potter makes a kind of stone. The pot may break, but the pieces or the sherds remain. So to pieces of Willow Pattern and coloured bowls and slipware and stoneware from round an old cottage of A.D. 1800 you can add scraps of pottery of 1800 B.C., scraps two thousand, three thousand, even four thousand years old – again if you look where you ought to look.

Like flints, pottery may be on the surface. Lorry loads must be scattered about over England, thrown up by moles, by weathering, by the plough, by anything which opens the ground an inch or two.

The first New Stone Age farmers in Britain made pots and vessels of clay. So did the Bronze Age peoples after them, and the Iron Age peoples later still. Gritty, grey or blackish or red or dark brown, scraps which are smooth or rough, scraps which are ornamented with dots and grooves and various patterns, lie about on the uplands, remains of vessels skilfully built up by hand without a potter's wheel, and then fired and hardened without a kiln.

URNS OF THE BRONZE AGE WHICH CONTAINED ASHES OF
THE DEAD

The potter's wheel came to England quite late in the Iron Age, not so long before the Romans. Bits of wheel-made pottery, of these later times and of the centuries when Britain was under the Romans, you can tell from their regularity, and from concentric lines in the surface. Usually they are thinner as well.

When you come across sherds with a glaze on them, you have moved nearer the cottage pottery, into the Middle Ages and later still.

Take the bits you collect (this really applies to the flints as well) to the museum, and compare them with specimens in the cases, which will be labelled and dated. And talk to the man in charge. He will help. He may even let you handle bits which are kept for study and comparison. Also he will know other good places to search.

One thing is important. Always treasure pieces of rim or base, or pieces which are patterned. These are the ones easiest to identify.

Something else, too, at the end of this collector's chapter.

In your district you will come to know the barrows, or burial mounds, of all shapes and kinds, the stone burial chambers which have lost their cover of earth, the menhirs or standing stones, the hill camps (mostly Iron Age, these camps are; belonging to a more quarrelsome time, when men had to defend themselves and their flocks and herds), the square Roman forts, the Roman roads and remnants, and the long earthen dykes with ditches which tell of trouble between the British and the invading Englishmen, after the Roman government had ended.

Excellent. But just to have inside you a still stronger and better feeling about death and life and man and your own ancestors and the way time passes, century after century, look into one miraculous book – *Urne-buriall*, by Sir Thomas Browne.

Sir Thomas Browne was a doctor in Norwich and, he wrote the five short, grand chapters of this book in 1658, when some urns and ashes from the late Bronze Age had been revealed in a sandy meadow in Norfolk.

Don't read every word, unless you want to. Skip and search and dig out the grandest passages.

Man is a noble animal, splendid in ashes and pompous in the grave.

But nothing lasts on earth, in spite of pyramids and urns and barrows:

In vain do individuals hope for immortality, or any patent from oblivion, in preservations below the moon.

Read such bits to yourself by yourself, aloud.

To be gnawed out of our graves, to have our skulls made drinking bowls and our bones turned into pipes, to delight and sport our enemies, are tragical abominations escaped in burning burials.

Urnal interments and burnt relicks lie not in fear of worms, or to be an heritage for serpents.

Another great writer said in a poem that Sir Thomas Browne makes all the past 'like coloured fireworks burn'; which is what the past should do.

I think all the archaeologists of England have been moved and encouraged by reading *Urne-buriall*.

Looking back at this chapter I think I should put some dates in the form of a table for keeping its very ancient matters as right as possible in the memory.

The glaciers have gone, the mammoths have disappeared, the Old Stone Age (Paleolithic) has ended and the Middle Stone Age (Meso-

lithic) of marshes and forests and the	*about*
drowning of the North Sea lands is	10,000 B.C.
beginning. The Dogger Bank Lands	*about*
go under the sea.	7000 B.C.
The English Channel cut and Eng-	*nearer*
land – or Britain – becomes an island.	6000 B.C.
	than
	7000 B.C.
The New Stone Age (Neolithic) the	
age of the first men in Britain who	
grew corn and bred animals for meat	*about*
and milk begins.	3000 B.C.
The Bronze Age of new settlers in	
Britain who still use flint and other	
hard stones, but make their weapons	*about*
and tools more and more of bronze,	1800 or
begins.	1900 B.C.
The Iron Age, of Celtic peoples who	
fight and work mostly with iron and	
build hill camps around Britain, be-	*about*
gins.	420 B.C.
The Romans, commanded by Claud-	
ius, invade Britain and begin the	
Roman conquest and settlement (this	
sounds too much like the history	*in*
period).	A.D. 43
Everything goes to pieces and the	
Roman power ends in Britain and	
the English begin to push their way	*about*
in.	A.D. 410

In this chapter flints and barrows and pottery have been the important things. Most facts which are known about barrows, who was buried in them, and how and when; and how to distinguish long-barrows, bowl-

barrows, bell-barrows, disc-barrows, saucer-barrows, and pond-barrows, are to be found in 'The Ancient Burial-Mounds of England',* by L. V. Grinsell (1953).

About pots and tools and weapons there are three books full of information and plates which you can buy from the British Museum, London, WC1. 'Flint Implements'** (1950), 'Later Prehistoric Antiquities'** (1953) about New Stone Age, Bronze Age, and Iron Age, and 'Antiquities of Roman Britain'**(1951).

These cost only 20p., 30p., and 50p.

From the British Museum (Natural History), London, SW1, Kenneth Oakley's 'Man the Toolmaker'** (only 20p.) tells you mainly about the tools men contrived in the Old Stone Age.

From the bookshops of the Stationery Office (in London, Edinburgh, Cardiff, Belfast, Manchester, Birmingham and Bristol), you can buy (12½p; and it is stuffed full with explorer's information) 'Field Archaeology, Some Notes for Beginners'.** Another book to read is 'Going into the Past'** by Gordon Copley (1955).

Probably your library will have 'Roman Roads in Britain', by I. D. Margary, 1967, from which you can learn how to recognize Roman roads, and how to find any length of road which has been recorded so far in Britain.

There are excellent guides to all the prehistoric remains worth visiting, 'Guide to Prehistoric England,* by Nicholas Thomas (1960), 'Guide to Prehistoric Scotland'* by Richard Feacham (1963), 'Prehistoric and Early Christian Ireland: A Guide',* by Estyn Evans (1966).

Also if you like to know more about the flint mines at

Grimes Graves in Norfolk, and about the modern flint knappers of Norfolk (twenty years ago they were still making gun flints for Africa), read 'In Breckland Wilds' (1937) by W. G. Clarke and R. Rainbird Clarke.

You will find information, too, about flint mines and about many things mentioned in this book and hundreds of other things you may come across throughout the British Isles, in a kind of dictionary or pocket encyclopaedia I have put together, with many illustrations: 'The Shell Country Alphabet'* by Geoffrey Grigson (1966).

And don't forget SIR THOMAS BROWNE.

9

ANY POETS?

SOME time ago a television reporter wanted to find out how much poetry we all knew. He stopped people in a London street, held a microphone up and said 'Can you remember any poets, and any poems? Can you quote any poems, do you know any poetry off by heart?'

Most of them couldn't remember very many, or quote very much. But nearly all of them retained inklings of one poem – which you perhaps remember better than they did – about daffodils, by William Wordsworth.

'I wandered lonely as a cloud' – yes, they remembered that, it seemed a nice idea, wandering lonely as a cloud.

They were not so strong on the next line, about the cloud floating over vales and hills. But they did remember how the daffodils came in:

> *When all at once I saw a crowd,*
> *A host, of golden daffodils;*
> *Beside the lake, beneath the trees*
> *Fluttering –*

Was that how it went? *Fluttering . . . ?* Yes, –

> *Fluttering and dancing in the breeze.*

I suppose they remembered the poem because of the way

it sounds and because, naturally, they liked daffodils.

But suppose one of those people on the street had come from Westmorland, from Cumberland, from the Lake District: he might have known the daffodil place which made William Wordsworth write the poem, he probably wouldn't have said *er, er, er,* into the microphone and the eye of the TV camera, he would have been able to say most of the poem, perhaps all of the poem, off by heart.

See what I am getting at. In this chapter – one I promised earlier on – I am suggesting it is a good thing to know about the poems and poets of places you are familiar with (especially if they are good poems, good poets, and good places) – places you are fond of (as the poets would have been) perhaps because you live there, were born or brought up there, or go there for holidays.

That daffodil poem by Wordsworth, like many others, is one you can pin down to a particular time, and a particular place. It is even known exactly what Wordsworth, or at any rate youngish Wordsworth's not very old sister, Dorothy, felt when they saw the wild daffodils nodding on that day and in that place.

Let's think. It was a Thursday, in April – April 15th, 1802. Dorothy Wordsworth put down everything about that day in her 'Grasmere Journal'. She was 30, a strange-looking girl, not very pretty or graceful, with wild eyes in a face as dark as a gypsy's, her brother William was 32, strong, with a tough, rather ugly face, coming out at you in a large long nose, though he usually looked as if he was just going to smile or laugh. They lived by themselves in a white cottage, which had been an inn called The Dove and Olive Branch, with a mountain behind them, and Grasmere, the lake, in front of them.

For a few days they had been staying with some

friends, some miles away over the mountains on another lake, Ullswater. This Thursday morning was misty, not very cold. In the afternoon they started home, and they found the wind almost too strong to walk against. They sheltered in a boat-house, they sheltered under a gorse

ULLSWATER

bush, walked on and sheltered in a lane, and noticed how rough the lake was. There was a boat in a bay by itself, showing the roughness of the lake by its movements. Then they climbed into a field to avoid some cows, found some primroses, wood-sorrel flowers, dog-violets, wild strawberry flowers and celandines by the road – you see the two Wordsworths were noticing everything – and *then*, some daffodils in a wood by the lake, only a few of them.

They thought the lake must have floated the seeds ashore, starting a little colony of daffodils. But they walked on and found there were hundreds, thousands more.

This is what Dorothy Wordsworth wrote down that night, when they were cosy at an inn at the far end of the lake, while it was still raining and blowing outside:

As we went along there were more and yet more; and at last, under the boughs of the trees, we saw that there was a long belt of them along the shore, about the breadth of a country turnpike road. I never saw daffodils so beautiful. They grew among the mossy stones about and about them; some rested their heads upon these stones as on a pillow for weariness; and the rest tossed and reeled and danced and seemed as if they verily laughed with the wind, that blew upon them over the lake; they looked so gay, ever glancing, ever changing. The wind blew directly over the lake to them. There was here and there a little knot, and a few stragglers a few yards higher up; but they were so few as not to disturb the simplicity, unity, and life of that one busy highway.

One busy highway of daffodils, one busy roadway of daffodils in a high wind.

They remembered that highway of daffodils; and then two years later, in 1804, Wordsworth made them into the poem those people in front of the TV microphone and camera could just remember, in 1969.

It would have been nice if the TV man could have said to them, 'Well, the daffodils are still fluttering and dancing where Wordsworth saw them' – as they are. (If you read the poem as well as Dorothy Wordsworth's description of the daffodils, you will see that William, in the poem says the daffodils were dancing in a *breeze*, and that Dorothy in her journal, says that a real high wind, a wind she and her brother had hardly been able to walk against, came straight off the lake on to the daffodils.

Wordsworth softened a gale to a breeze when he wrote the poem two years after their walk, thinking more about the pleasure they had been given by the wild daffodils than the unpleasantness they had felt in that cold strong wind.)

I do not say you can often pin down a wonderful poem to a day and a place. Still, it is possible, sometimes.

But first you have to pin down your poets, the ones whose lives have made them a part of your countryside – other writers as well as poets, such as Gilbert White of Hampshire (Chapter 2) and Sir Thomas Browne of Norfolk (Chapter 8); but poets in particular, because poems stay so alive. They keep the poets who wrote them so alive, the poets who shared, perhaps hundreds of years ago, and loved, the places or the county you love today, in your time.

County guidebooks help you to the names. Some of the old *Murray's Hand-books* I recommended in Chapter 2 have lists, at the beginning, of each county's 'Prominent Men' or 'Eminent Natives'. A little more up to date are the small red *Little Guides*. A few of these you can buy in modern editions; most of them, out of print (another way of saying no longer obtainable new), you can buy secondhand without trouble; and certainly these *Little Guides* will be found in your local library. Nearly all of them start off with a roll of the notable men and women belonging to the county.

Suppose your county is Suffolk. The *Little Guide* to Suffolk, one of the modern ones, tells you that Suffolk poets include:

John Lydgate, monk of St Edmund's Abbey at Bury.

Henry Howard, Earl of Surrey, whose head was cut off in 1547.

Thomas Nashe, who was three years younger than Shakespeare, and wrote one – just one – of the best poems in English.

George Crabbe, poet of the North Sea coast.

Edward Fitzgerald, who rewrote the Persian poet Omar Khayyám in English.

Quite a haul. Let's look at them, one by one.

JOHN LYDGATE (who lived from about 1370 to about 1451). If you go to Lidgate village, between Clare and Newmarket, you can see the house he was born in, and in Lidgate church you can see what is supposed to be the brass of this John of Lidgate, or John from Lidgate. Books say he is rather a dull poet, who goes on and on. This is not entirely true. It does not take much trouble to find lines by John Lydgate which show him enjoying the world just as we do, looking at the moon:

> *And as I stood myself alloone, upon the New Year night,*
> *I prayed unto the frosty moon, with her pale light,*
> *To go and recomaunde me unto my lady dear,*

or getting up early in the morning in May:

> *I rose anon and thought I woulde gone*
> *Unto the wood to hear the birdes sing*
> *When that the misty vapour was agone*
> *And clear and fair was the morwenyng.*
> *The dew also like silver in shining.*

JOHN LYDGATE, OFFERING A BOOK TO HIS PATRON, WITH
A PILGRIM

In Bury St Edmunds you might think of him, in his sandals and the black robes or 'habit' of a young Benedictine monk, going in and out of the great gates of his abbey (which are still there).

HENRY HOWARD, Earl of Surrey: you can see him – this is uncommon for a poet – carved in alabaster, feet on a lion, lying next to his wife, on a grand tomb among other grand tombs of his lineage, in the church at Framlingham. The castle at Framlingham, in ruins, was one of his homes when he was a child. When he was a boy he was Cupbearer to Henry VIII; he went with Henry VIII to the Field of the Cloth of Gold, and Henry VIII had him executed for high treason.

Rather a rowdy man. His poems – no, not very good; though he wrote a nice one when he was in prison for a while in Windsor Castle, recalling that in his childhood in the castle he and the king's son would hover round the large green courtyards and miss the ball at tennis because they kept on looking up to the girls' windows.

THOMAS NASHE. There isn't much to say about him as a Suffolk man, or a man of East Anglia, except that an East Anglian he was, born at Lowestoft in 1567; and that he wrote some fun – prose fun – in praise of Yarmouth red herrings. (Red herrings are not a joke, by the way. They are herrings smoked very hard and red, and tasty, still produced in Yarmouth and exported to poor people in Africa, Greece, Italy, South America and the West Indies.) He was a grand knockabout writer in Shakespeare's London, a master of words, who in his short life wrote a great litany poem, every verse chiming.

> *I am sick, I must die*
> *Lord, have mercy on us!*

It was about the Plague bringing everybody to death and dust:

> *Beauty is but a flower*
> *Which wrinkles will devour;*
> *Brightness falls from the air,*
> *Queens have died young and fair,*
> *Dust hath closed Helen's eye.*
> *I am sick, I must die*
> *Lord, have mercy on us!*

GILES FLETCHER – he was a clergyman (like many poets in earlier centuries), rector of Alderton, marshy, willowy parish along the North Sea, where he is buried in the

church, and where nobody appreciated him. 'His clown-
ish and low-parted parishioners (having nothing but
their shoes high about them) valued not their pastor
according to his worth, which disposed him to mel-
ancholy, and hastened his dissolution', poor Giles Fletcher dying when he was still quite young, in 1623.

Perhaps he had malaria, which was common then in
marshy parts of Suffolk. Ague or malaria was put down
in old days, not to mosquitoes biting you and infecting
you with an organism, but to breathing bad air (which is
what malaria means, no more than *mal aria*, bad air, in
Italian), and Suffolk was said to have the best and worst
air in England – 'best about Bury, and worst on the sea-
side where Master Fletcher was beneficed' (i.e. where he
was clergyman). He wrote a long luscious poem partly
about saints in heaven where

> *No losse, no griefe, no change waites on their winged
> hours.*

Sad Alderton was no heaven.

GEORGE CRABBE – he grew up in a sad poor way also on
Suffolk's North Sea, at Aldeburgh, where he was born in
1754, not very far from Giles Fletcher's Alderton rec-
tory. His poems are sad, too, sad and splendid sometimes
at once. They are full of storms and glitter and danger,
and there are enough of them to explore for years. Sometimes in his poems there are black clouds over the North
Sea, sometimes people walk along the Suffolk shore in
sunshine, looking for red pebbles, jelly-fish, pearl-shells
and starfish, and watching the ships 'in the sleepy sea'.
Also, since he took opium as a medicine, he had to
endure terrible dreams. Fiends came and spiked him on
the Northern Lights, they hung him on top of trees, on

the thin twigs at the very top, they fixed him on sand-banks, with the tide rising up to his mouth and nose to drown him – and then turning just in time; or they fixed him in a quaking fen:

> *Those fiends upon a shaking fen*
> *Fix'd me in dark tempestuous night;*
> *There never trod the foot of men,*
> *There flock'd the fowl in wint'ry flight;*
> *There danced the moor's deceitful light*
> *Above the pool where sedges grow;*
> *And when the morning-sun shone bright,*
> *It shone upon a field of snow!*

(Someone else who lives at Aldeburgh is Benjamin Britten the composer, a great admirer of Crabbe. He is a Suffolk man, and was born – like Thomas Nashe – at Lowestoft.)

EDWARD FITZGERALD, last of our five Suffolk poets, 'Old Fitz' (that was what his friend Tennyson called him) from Woodbridge, who loved to read Crabbe's poems, and to come down and walk on the cliffs at Dunwich, where Suffolk crumbles a yard into the sea every year, and where bones tumble down to the shingle from old graveyards. A real Suffolk man, born Edward Purcell (he changed later to his Irish name), in 1809, at Bredfield near Woodbridge. For more than a hundred years now people all over the world have been reading his English version of *The Rubáiyát of Omar Khayyám*:

> *They say the Lion and the Lizard keep*
> *The Courts where Jamshyd gloried and drank*
> * deep;*
> *And Bahrám, that great Hunter – the Wild Ass*
> *Stamps o'er his Head, but cannot break his Sleep.*

Probably you don't come from Suffolk, probably you don't live there or go there. So you may think it unfair to give so many words to five Suffolk poets. But it shows, you may have five poets as good or better, or more than five poets, for your county. Or you may have none. But look and see. (And don't forget that if you come from Warwickshire how unfair it is to have Shakespeare to yourself – and another great Warwickshire poet, W. H. Auden – that Wystan Hugh Auden, who was brought up in the Birmingham suburbs, and was named, you remember, after a Shropshire or Leicestershire saint.)

Not to go through all the counties, here are just a few more:

Devonshire has Sir Walter Ralegh, George Peele, John Ford, William Browne of Tavistock, Herrick, John Gay (who wrote *The Beggar's Opera*), Coleridge (who wrote *Kubla Khan*).

Essex has William Morris and Gerard Manley Hopkins.

Herefordshire has Traherne.

Kent has Sir Thomas Wyatt, Sir Philip Sidney, Christopher Marlowe, Sir Richard Lovelace, Christopher Smart (do you remember? Page 26).

Lincolnshire has Tennyson.

London has scores.

Northamptonshire has John Dryden and John Clare (that is a good pair).

Northumberland has Swinburne.

And just thinking back to Norfolk (because it is Suffolk's neighbour and rival), it doesn't do half as well

as Suffolk. The only real poets I can think of from Norfolk are John Skelton and William Cowper (and other
counties can claim more of Cowper).

Still, to Norfolk belongs – who?

SIR THOMAS BROWNE, once more

(And if he isn't a poet, he did write one or two poems.)

*When you have pinned down your poets, where do you
find the poems?*

*The first answer is anthologies. Try first of all the
Oxford books – the 'Oxford Book of Sixteenth Century
Verse', the Oxford Books of Seventeenth, and Eighteenth, and Nineteenth Century Verse. Then look
through the rest of the poetry shelves in the library.*

*And of course a first place to look, again in the library,
for the poets' lives, and where they lived, is that great
'Dictionary of National Biography' I have spoken of
before.*

10

FOSSILS, SKULLS, SHELLS

I WANT an excuse for this new chapter. Here is a book which is not, as you know, about birds and their eggs or about butterflies or moths or beetles or wild flowers. It is not about natural history, but mostly about things made by man, in the past.

And here I am wanting an excuse for deserting man, and going back further in time in search of fossils, which are natural history; then I need to say a word about collecting skulls, which are natural history as well; and (natural history for a third time) I am all for walking along the edges of the sea – or into the junk shop in the town – after shells.

My excuse is that shells and fossils and skulls are all of them hard collectable objects. Also that shells and fossils have delighted men all over the world for thousands upon thousands of years.

Old Stone Age men upwards of 20,000 or 30,000 B.C. collected sea-shells and have been found buried under the floor of their caves along with the shells they wore round their heads, round their necks, or round their waists. In 1823 an Oxford geologist found the Red Lady of Paviland (really she was not a woman, but a young huntsman of the Old Stone Age) in a cave in the limestone cliffs of Gower, near Paviland Farm, in South Wales. She – or he – had been buried in red ochre, perhaps because it was the colour of the blood of life, with shells, and also with the skull of a mammoth along-side. In the wonderful University Museum at Oxford (wonderful, because it is quite unlike any other museum you can find in the British Isles, crowded and full of surprises) you can see some of those shells as well as the red bones of the owner.

As for fossils, in the Bronze Age fossil sea-urchins were sometimes part of the store of things put near the remains of the dead in barrows.

Fossils were puzzling objects, as well. Two hundred years ago men were still asking what they had been, or more exactly what they were. And where had they come from? How had they been made? Were they related in some way to weapons of flint and stone? Some people thought they must be. Both fossils and stone weapons had been made, they suggested, by a creative power in the soil and in the rocks. Others thought that arrow-heads and stone axes must have been thunderbolts (a bolt is an arrow) which fell out of the beetling clouds of a thunderstorm; or if that was not so, they must be weapons which had fallen down from those heavenly battles at the end of which Satan and his wicked angels had been cast from heaven into hell. Others considered that weapons of stone had been made and used by the demons and the goblins – by pucks, thyrsts, hobs, bugs, and all the wicked company of elves – for one purpose, shooting illnesses at men or at men's cows and horses and pigs.

One Scottish witch named Isobel Gowdie, when she was tried in 1662, even declared she had seen elf-boys whittling elf-arrows or flint arrowheads 'with a sharp thing lyk a pakyng needle'.

Men believed that evil creatures had also whittled and sharpened some of the commonest of chalk fossils, the belemnites; which are really the fossilized tips of the inside shells of extinct kinds of cuttle-fish. *Belemnon* in Greek means a dart or an arrow. And in English belemnites were commonly called bolt-heads or elf-bolts. Not surprising, when you pull a belemnite out of a chalk cliff and consider how regular it is and how sharp.

Since this is not a natural history book, I am not going to say much about different kinds. But I do urge you to keep your eyes skinned when you come to quarries or cliffs or cuttings or banks of streams — even when you come face to face with a wall made of a stone which itself is made up of fossils.

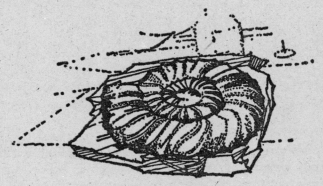

FOSSIL AMMONITE

As for liking fossils, they can be studied as a scientist studies them, because they are relics of ancient life, animal or vegetable; they can be enjoyed because they look queer or look beautiful, or because some of them have been so strangely associated with our remote ancestors.

Why, for instance, were a hundred or so fossil sea-urchins put round a crouched burial of a woman and a child inside a barrow on the Dunstable Downs, in Bedfordshire? The answer (I suspect) may be hidden inside a country name for fossil sea-urchins, which is fairy loaves. It is a country belief that you can never want for bread as long as you own a fairy loaf. Perhaps with all those fairy loaves round them the woman and her child under the barrow would never want for bread or food in their spirit life.

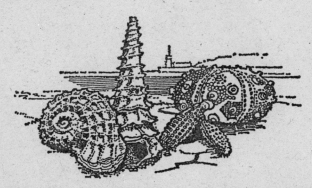

FOSSILS, TWO SHELLS, SEA-URCHIN, AND ITS SPINES

I don't myself know many better excitements than finding pieces of fossilized coral from an ancient coral reef; or coming across a large ammonite flat in its ancient position in the bed of an old limestone quarry; or picking up on beaches in Dorset tiny ammonites transformed into brassy gleaming iron pyrites, which have been washed out of the grey cliffs of shale and cleaned and polished by the sand and the tide.

And skulls. Wild skulls make a good collection, not as difficult to begin or add to as you might expect. Fox and badger skulls outside the earths are the first to go for – and when possible, you want your skulls whole, lower jaw included, with all the teeth, upper and lower.

Think: badger, fox, otter (that's a problem), hare, rabbit (not so many of them about), stoat, weasel, squir-

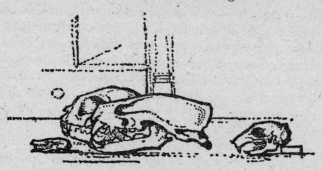

SKULLS: MOLE, CAT, OTTER, SQUIRREL

rel – and still you won't have come near the skulls of a grey seal, a porpoise, a dolphin (I once had a dolphin skull, with its long beak, filled with teeth like a saw, from a beach in the Isles of Scilly) – let alone the snakes. Or the bats.

You can add to your skulls the antlers of the various

RED DEER ANTLERS

deer – red deer, roe deer, fallow deer. I do not see why you should end with 'wild skulls'. What about horse, cattle, sheep, goat, and the rest of them? It should be a rule, though, that your skulls, all of them, wild and tame, should be ready prepared for you, more or less. They should be found in the open, cleaned and picked off by nature, wind, rain, maggot and beetle. No murder beforehand.

A human skull? Well, it is a possibility. I once bought one in a shop off High Holborn in London for five shillings. But I wasn't allowed to keep it.

Shells. If you know what I mean, shells are almost human objects. We might have invented them. They are strange, they are beautiful, they do not seem at all

A VARIETY OF SHELLS

deathly or dismal, and they gleam and glitter like life or poems or sunshine. Anyhow, the life inside them has gone; and as a collector of pleasant things (and not a marine biologist) you hardly miss it.

Everyone should be a beachcomber, when he has the chance. Everyone should parade the beaches and turn over the tide wrack for the things which are washed ashore. For shells, go beachcombing, like that islander who found the chessmen, after a good furious storm.

JUNK SHOP

And remember there are beaches – or beaches and cliffs together (as along the Dorset coast or along Robin Hood's Bay in Yorkshire) which offer the double gifts of fossil and shell.

But beaches and cliffs are not the only places to search. Keep that eye of yours on junk shops, second-hand shops, shops which have trays and tables outside. Shops where they sell everything from derelict type-writers to gaping wireless sets and dead dynamos and broken dominoes and battered saucepans and old walking-sticks and hat-boxes and thrillers with the paper jackets half torn away.

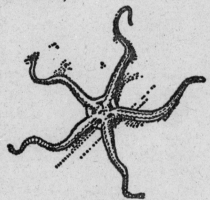

FOSSIL STARFISH

Once in a Wiltshire town I picked a way through all the rubbish in a shop like that to a battered mahogany cabinet. Every drawer was full of shells. They were going for twopence, sixpence, a shilling apiece. Someone had collected them about 1800; and they had come to that dismal shop from all the seas and shores of the world – the Gulf of Venice, the Red Sea, Malabar, the Coast of Coromandel, the Island of Aboyna and Surinam and Barbados and Cayenne and Barbary. Their names (I know them all, because I bought the catalogue, carefully written out and bound in vellum), their collectors' names of the eighteenth century and the nineteenth century, were no less wonderful. The Pagoda, the Persian Harp, and the Persian Robe, the Gondola, the Ethiopian Crown, the Flambeaux, the Porcelain, the Tulip Wedge, the Watering Pot, the Broad Striped Zebra, the Ducal Mantle, and so on.

Junk shops are the place for fossils out of old cabinets or boxes, as well as for shells. Also for pieces of crystal and pieces of ore, and cut and polished pieces of coloured stone – even, now and again, for a fine flint dagger or a stone axe.

Sometimes a faded label still tells the name of the object and where it was found. Save the labels, stick them on afresh or write them out afresh, if need be, adding where *you*, as well, made your find; and the date.

When you bring them home, and get busy with a little soap and warm water, how shells, minerals, crystals, pieces of ore come to life and light and colour – often colour you did not suspect!

So this is the place for a poem about people and shells – very short, like most Japanese poems – which one of the greatest of all painters Hokusai (who lived from 1760 to 1849) added to the corner of one of his colour prints:

> *Girls with sweet voices go to Susaki*
> *Shore at the ebb of the tide for shells –*
> *For fishes and shells.*
> *O like the flower-shells in the foam,*
> *They gather and crowd by the sea.*

As for pieces of ore and crystal, it is always worth

looking around old mine dumps, especially in Cornwall and Derbyshire. Here and there in Cornwall there are veins of glittering ore running down a cliff.

Fossils are stony prints or transformations of living things throughout millions of years. So there are thousands and thousands of kinds.

That means you cannot have a convenient handy guide to the fossils of Britain, as you can to the flowers of Britain or British butterflies.

A small 'Young Naturalist's book', 'British Fossils',** by Duncan Forbes (1951) tells you something, with a chapter about collecting. Also try 'Exploring the Rocks'** by Christopher Trent (1957).

From one of the Stationery Offices or Edward Stanford, Ltd (see page 20) you can buy the pamphlet for your district in the 'British Regional Geology'** series. These pamphlets are made by officers of the Geological Survey, and they may tell you quite a bit about fossils – also about mines, quarries, etc. Also there may be a bigger (but much more expensive) Geological Memoir about your neighbourhood.

For 37½p from the Palaeontological Society, Burlington House, London, W1, you can buy a 'Directory of British Fossiliferous Localities'** (1954), arranged county by county.

I hope your luck with this directory will be better than mine. I consulted it, and decided to go to three quarries. Two were filled up, one was nearly filled up – with old tins and bottles when I expected sea-urchins.

Minerals and the like are difficult to reduce to a book or to useful descriptions. Still, a buyable inexpensive small book which will help, is 'The Observer's Book of British Geology'** by I. O. Evans (1953) – with a chapter, as well, about fossils.

As for skulls, quite a bit is to be learned and many illustrations are to be had in 'A Beast Book for the Pocket', by Edmund Sandars (1937). From the British Museum (Natural History) London, SW1, 'A List of British Mammals',** by T. C. S. Morrison-Scott (1952), will tell you a good deal about skulls. Many skulls are very accurately drawn in 'Bones for the Archaeologist', by I. W. Cornwall (1956), but it is an expensive book, and may not be in the local library.

Shells. Look at 'Shell Life', by Edward Step, and 'Collins Pocket Guide to the Sea Shore', by J. H. Barratt and C. M. Yonge. Also 'Shells on the Seashore', by Philip Street.

If you want to make shell patterns, round, in squares, rectangles, etc., out of the periwinkles and winkles and small cowries and tellins from the beach, you can easily make them on holiday by pressing the shells into plasticine.

For permanent shell patterns you need plaster of Paris or one of the pink plasters you can buy from builder's merchants by the pound. Don't forget how quickly these plasters set. It will be best to work your pattern out first on the plasticine.

Also don't try to turn shells into something else – little birds, men, dogs, heaven knows what. It is like electric fires which pretend to be coal; and it is an insult to the shell, which is beautiful in itself.

Since we are talking of beaches and shells, if you ever want to mount and dry seaweeds, you should float your seaweed in a bowl of water, slip paper underneath it, arrange the seaweed over the paper very carefully with a darning-needle and a paint-brush, and then lift it carefully out. Put a piece of thin cloth on the top of the seaweed, and then press and dry the seaweed and the paper together between sheets of blotting paper or newspaper.

11

THE CABINET OF CURIOSITIES,
THE TEMPLE OF THE MUSES,
OR YOUR OWN MUSEUM

IN a book for boys I read that if the boys keep their own museum, they should make it as much like a real museum as possible: it shouldn't be too mixed a collection, it should be serious, it shouldn't be a museum of curios.

But why? Why shouldn't it contain curious things? And why should a real museum be more real than any museum you decide to have? Also why should a museum be for boys more than for girls?

I say the museum should be a family affair. Your father and mother should be its patrons – and they should be contributors as well (under your direction and discretion).

As for what should be in it, once when I was beach-combing along an Atlantic beach, with no land between me and America, I found an old boot, which had been thrown very high up by a more than usually high spring tide. It was a golden boot. It was entirely covered with golden lichen.

I should like that boot in my museum – if only the lichen would not die – as much as an axe-head, or a mammoth's tooth or a green tropical beetle.

Everything which entertains you; everything which is special and curious, deserves a place in your museum. It is where you should put all things you are glad to find or glad to be given. Your museum is your Temple of the Muses, which is what 'museum' means, and the Muses were goddesses concerned with the delights, especially, of poetry and history.

Put in your museum things which feel to you to have poetry in them, and history in them as well.

Curious is the word. Early museums all began – and quite right – as Cabinets of Curiosities or Rarities. That is how the greatest of all museums, the British Museum, began. Sir Hans Sloane, a doctor in London, started collecting when he was young. When he was old, he had collected more than fifty thousand curiosities, or curios for short – corals, crystals, shells, minerals, coins, fossils, plants, butterflies, fishes, a rhinoceros, and 'miscellaneous things', as he called them in his catalogue.

I think Sir Hans liked that canticle which comes far too seldom on Sunday morning, the *Benedicite Omnia Opera*, in which everything – sun, moon, stars, showers, dew, winds, frost, ice, snow, nights and days and light and darkness and lightnings and clouds, mountains and hills and green things, and wells, seas, floods, whales, fowls of the air, beasts, cattle, children of men, and Ananias, Azarias and Misael – is told to bless and praise and magnify.

Sir Hans in his long wig would have had them all in his museum or cabinet (which overfilled the whole of his house near Sloane Square – a square named after him) – if he could; and when he died at last, he left every one of his curiosities to be bought by Parliament.

So they became the British Museum – in 1753.

Two of Sir Hans's curiosities were 'The Hat of the Patriarch of China made of Canes split on the outside and lin'd with Plantain Leaves' and a very famous flint hand-axe which was found with the bones of a mammoth in London, near Gray's Inn. Sir Hans thought it was a spearhead used – which explained the mammoth bones – by a British warrior against an elephant corps of the Romans when they invaded Britain in A.D. 43.

Go ahead. Your Museum of Curiosities is your own. It is for your excitement. It is to be your own Box of Delights. Let it include a rattlesnake's rattle, a dried seahorse, and a coin in lava – and Sir Hans Sloane's wig, if you can find it. Early Cabinets of Curiosities or Rarities liked especially to own the horn of a unicorn and pieces of mermaid; and other things which never existed.

You want room – and you want a table to work on, and shelves, and trays and boxes and a magnifying glass.

You want a catalogue or register – a notebook in which you can register and describe each one of your finds or gifts as soon as it is added to the museum. It will be as well to keep that register handy on a string. The important things need labelling with name and date and where they came from. Better still, you can write *on* them – since labels fall off and get mixed or lost. Write where the writing does not show (in big museums, even the British Museum, they sometimes write names and numbers right across very attractive things); and use washable inks, black for marking light objects, white for marking the dark ones.

Half the point and much of the pleasure of the museum is to be able to see things at a glance. So don't tuck everything away, keep as much as possible ON EXHIBITION.

Where? On shelves, on trays, on squares or rectangles of plaster board, or any board which is fairly firm, yet soft enough to take pins. Suppose you have near you (as we have in my family) a site where Roman pottery can be picked up. Mount your series of sherds from that one site on the same piece of board, with pins. This is better than using glue. If you glue them, it is not so easy to take the sherds off again and examine both sides.

A square of plaster board would also do very well for a series of old clay pipes or bottle seals, and for much else.

Even that is not enough. A friend of mine who is a sculptor owns some special pottery figures from Mexico and from the Greek islands, some of them hundreds, some of them thousands of years old, as well as a few carvings from Africa. He wants the best of them to be seen no less than the larger things which he carves himself. They are too precious to have on the mantelpiece or anywhere else where they could be knocked down.

So he has contrived what should not be impossible in your own museum, for your own extra-specials – small shelves on the wall, like bookcases, each with a glass door; but each with a bar of electric light inside.

Old trays are worth having, repainted white and clean, so long as you have places to put them on. For instance, you can use a tray to exhibit strange objects from a beach, whether shells or dry sea-stars, or fragments of glass moulded by the sea, or pebbles of beautiful colour and shape; all those things you are tempted to bring back, and then do not know what to do with.

Next, why not make your museum an art gallery as well? Your parents *may* not mind if you paste pictures on the museum walls – pictures out of newspapers and magazines which you fancy or which have to do with your museum quest.

Probably they will mind still less if you pin things up or fix them up with small pieces of Sellotape. So collect postcards (coloured ones) of great pictures or gay pictures by good artists, ancient and modern, from all the art galleries of the world.

I think it is rather more civilized than stamp-collecting (which just happens to be the most organized kind of collecting, with the greatest number of shops and dealers).

Collect only the pictures you like. Try to discover from books in the library something about the men who painted them. Don't think there is something funny about the 'modern' pictures. They are often the gayest; and a picture after all, is painted to look exciting. It is something made of colours. You do not look at a goldfish or at a bunch of primroses and ask what it means.

The gay postcards round the museum will often look gayer still if they are sprayed first with a fixative or very thinly covered with gum arabic.

Now last of all, if you have a spare map of your district, pin that up, too. And your books should be handy, the kinds of books I have mentioned, and your natural history books as well (of course, many of your natural history finds have their place in the museum).

Also I rather think that the museum room, whether it is a bedroom, a playroom, a converted outhouse, really should be the place for all your odds and ends of apparatus, your sketchbooks and notebooks, your field-glasses, your walking-sticks (it is a good thing to make your own walking-sticks – from all kinds of wood, holly, white-thorn, blackthorn, hazel, even gorse); everything to do with collecting, looking and finding, down to your haversack and, if you have one, your vasculum, or plant-collecting tin, usually of aluminium; which is exceedingly useful, with its shoulder-strap and convenient shape, whether you collect plants or no.

About coloured postcards of pictures. Look the artists up by name in the encyclopaedias in your nearest library;

or in a big dictionary of art. The older artists will be included; but, since even new encyclopaedias can be a bit fusty, you will not find all of the modern ones. Look for them in 'A Dictionary of Modern Painting',* by Carlton Lake and Robert Maillard (1956), a small book and a nice one to own, but expensive.

A LAST WORD ABOUT BOOKS

I SAID I would remind you about books and Chapter 2. Having now reached the end, you might look back at Chapter 2, and have another glance at the bibliographical pieces in italic type at the end of each chapter.

Remember what I said about the small stars against some of the books and do make a list of all the books marked in that way, because I consider that they are the ones specially worth having in your own possession, on your museum bookshelf.

Some are cheap, some are not. I have not starred extremely expensive ones, though I have double-starred cheaper ones.

Remember about dearer books that if you get two or three book tokens for Christmas or a birthday, you can blow them together on one book.

Books with older dates after them may be ones the publisher can no longer supply. These, and even some of the later ones, you may be able to buy cheaper secondhand. Secondhand booksellers (perhaps it is wiser, after all, to call them 'antiquarian booksellers': they do not like the word 'secondhand', which suggests old clothes) will always try to obtain a book they do not have in stock; and they will tell you roughly what it will cost. Secondhand books cannot be bought with book tokens.

Coins. Many things you might collect for yourself and your museum I have mentioned, but I have hardly said a word about coins. A sensible book is Coin Collecting, by J. G. Milne, C. H. V. Sutherland, and J. D. A. Thompson (1950). And write to B. A. Seaby Ltd, 65 Great Portland St, London, W1. They are famous coin dealers, they publish good catalogues, and they like to help.

Some quite old coins are much less expensive than you might think – or might guess from the prices sometimes asked in a junk shop or curiosity shop where they know nothing about them.

Once more, don't forget Sir Thomas Browne:

To be gnaw'd out of our graves, to have our sculs made drinking-bowls, and our bones turned into Pipes, to delight and sport our Enemies, are Tragicall abominations, escaped in burning Burials . . .

Time which antiquates Antiquities . . .

There is no antidote against the Opium of time, which temporally considereth all things; Our Fathers find their graves in our short memories, and sadly tell us how we may be buried in our Survivors. Gravestones tell truth scarce forty years: Generations passe while some trees stand, and old Families last not three Oaks.

THE BLACK PEARL *by Scott O'Dell*   20p

552 52008 X   Carousel Fiction

The Black Pearl belonged to the old men, with legends and
stories to tell to pass the time – or so Ramon Salazar had
thought, until he came face to face with the devilfish and the
struggle for the pearl began. But Ramon had more than the
dangers of the sea to conquer. Others wanted the Great Pearl
of Heaven, including the evil Pearler from Seville.

TRUE MYSTERIES *by Bob Hoare*   25p

552 54009 9   Carousel Non-Fiction

Tales of the unknown, stories of people who suddenly appear
and disappear without explanation, and strange events which
present no logical answer, sometimes turning legend into
fact, or fact into legend. And always leaving a question mark.

HOW AND WHY WONDER BOOKS OF OUR EARTH
                                                        20p

552 86513 3

Despite Man's venture into outer space, the Planet Earth is
still the home of all known peoples. Our solar system may
provide a planet of alternative accommodation, but most of
us will continue to live on Earth. We should know as much
about our planet home as we can. OUR EARTH explains
how it was made and how it is changing all the time. A
scientific companion to the Carousel series EVERYDAY
LIFE IN PREHISTORIC TIMES.

CAROUSEL NON-FICTION PAPERBACK SERIES